PRAISE FOR *CONVINCE ME*

In *Convince Me*, Massey and Gambardella offer a fresh look at the art of persuasion. By blending the tactics of hostage negotiation with the finest of public relations, they have created a valuable guide for anyone keen to broaden and deepen their persuasive powers.

—**Daniel H. Pink**, #1 *New York Times* bestselling author of *To Sell Is Human*, *The Power of Regret*, and *When*

If you want to become impossible to say no to, read this book. You'll find tactics to be convincing you've never heard of before.

—**Jason Feifer**, author of *Build for Tomorrow* and editor in chief of *Entrepreneur Magazine*

Just 20 minutes with this book and it will change the way you think about selling. This is an essential book for anyone in sales . . . and everyone is in sales.

—**Joe Pulizzi**, author and founder of Content Marketing World

CONVINCE ME

CONVINCE ME

HIGH-STAKES NEGOTIATION TACTICS TO GET RESULTS IN ANY BUSINESS SITUATION

ADELE GAMBARDELLA
CHIP MASSEY

New York Chicago San Francisco Athens London
Madrid Mexico City Milan New Delhi
Singapore Sydney Toronto

1 2 3 4 5 6 7 8 9 LCR 28 27 26 25 24 23

ISBN 978-1-265-04757-3
MHID 1-265-04757-X

e-ISBN 978-1-265-04902-7
e-MHID 1-265-04902-5

Library of Congress Cataloging-in-Publication Data

Names: Gambardella, Adele, author. | Massey, Chip, author.
Title: Convince me : high-stakes negotiation tactics to get results in any business situation / Adele Gambardella and Chip Massey.
Description: New York : McGraw Hill, [2024] | Includes bibliographical references and index.
Identifiers: LCCN 2023016761 (print) | LCCN 2023016762 (ebook) | ISBN 9781265047573 (hardback) | ISBN 9781265049027 (ebook)
Subjects: LCSH: Negotiation in business. | Persuasion (Psychology)
Classification: LCC HD58.6 .G36 2024 (print) | LCC HD58.6 (ebook) | DDC 658.4/052—dc23/eng/20230601
LC record available at https://lccn.loc.gov/2023016761
LC ebook record available at https://lccn.loc.gov/2023016762

McGraw Hill books are available at special quantity discounts to use as premiums and sales promotions or for use in corporate training programs. To contact a representative, please visit the Contact Us pages at www.mhprofessional.com.

McGraw Hill is committed to making our products accessible to all learners. To learn more about the available support and accommodations we offer, please contact us at accessibility@mheducation.com. We also participate in the Access Text Network (www.accesstext.org), and ATN members may submit requests through ATN.

CONTENTS

INTRODUCTION

CONVINCING: THE ULTIMATE GAME-CHANGER

"We have your daughter. Pay up or she dies!" The caller slammed down the phone. Maria Sanchez was desperate. A real-life gang of "coyotes" smuggling undocumented immigrants into the United States from Mexico were holding Sanchez's 19-year-old daughter Rosa in a secret "hostage barn." An undocumented immigrant herself, Maria had already exhausted her meager savings paying the ransom. Now the kidnappers were demanding even more money. If she called the police, the hostage taker warned, she would never see her daughter again. Maria knew she lacked the skill, influence, and ability to save her daughter. At the considerable risk of jeopardizing her own place in the United States, she contacted the FBI.

CHIP MASSEY

No, this isn't the plot of a movie. This is a story from my former life. I'm Chip Massey, a former FBI negotiator and coauthor of this book. To help Maria get her daughter back, the bureau sent me and my team.

Hostage negotiators are more convincing than any salesperson you'll ever meet for one simple reason: we are dealing with real-life do-or-die situations. I had no personal connection to Maria—which isn't her real name, by the way. It wasn't my daughter whose life was at stake. Yet I knew exactly what Maria needed to say to the hostage taker to get her daughter freed. Maria's passion wouldn't be enough to save her daughter. She needed *know-how*—the kind of know-how that comes with a hostage negotiator's mastery of convincing techniques.

I prepared Maria for the next call, coaching her on exactly how to interact with her daughter's captor. I sat silently by Maria's side as she got on the phone with the kidnapper to work out a deal—a deal that was, in fact, a trap. Maria kept the kidnapper on the line as my team and I passed her notes, detailing exactly what to say. Every word she spoke had been strategically chosen to gain a tactical advantage. We wanted to slow down the negotiations and incrementally build trust. Seventy-three hours and 14 phone calls later, Maria's daughter and 22 other hostages were freed, and the coyote and his accomplices were in custody.

What if you could acquire these kinds of high-level convincing skills and apply them to your interactions with customers, prospects, colleagues, or the board of directors . . . pretty much anyone you need to convince about anything? If you think you must attend Quantico to acquire these skills, consider this: Maria is not a native English speaker. She was under extreme emotional strain and she was negotiating with a hardened criminal. Yet the skill set and techniques I taught her in a matter of hours empowered her to rescue her daughter in under three days!

The purpose of this book is to make you as convincing as you can possibly be. To take your convincing skills to the highest level. To truly transform you into someone who can convince others easily and quickly. Along the way, you will be given a window into the inner workings of some of the most convincing people on the planet, revealing what they did and how to apply their strategies to your own life. And you won't be learning from just me. I'll let my coauthor, Adele Gambardella, introduce herself.

ADELE GAMBARDELLA

As a crisis communications expert, I've conducted my share of high-stakes negotiations, both as the president of my own company and as a hired gun. I have trained Fortune 500 executives and consulted for US presidents and CEOs, using tried-and-true tactics that helped business superstars grow their empires. I've frequently been called to comment and weigh in on corporate scandals as a contributor to the *Wall Street Journal* and *Inc.* magazine. And I, too, have certain tricks of my trade that I have put to good use over the course of my career—things you don't necessarily learn at Quantico.

Together, Chip and I will share our different skill sets with you. Even though we have both worked and functioned in different worlds, we have both been in the convincing business all along. Our respective professional effectiveness depends on our ability to get people to trust us, work with us, and ultimately, do what we want them to do.

While you might think the skills of an FBI negotiator and a corporate communicator are very different, they have many similarities. Realizing how complementary our skill sets were, and how much we could learn from each other, Chip and I decided to form the Convincing Company. Our business today is teaching our powerful convincing strategies to companies, nonprofits, and C-suite executives who want to refine their powers of persuasion to get their way—and get ahead.

Our goal for this book is to teach you techniques and strategies that will give you the confidence, courage, and commitment to go after your biggest goals, without hesitation or self-doubt. Along the way, we'll give you a window into the inner workings of some of the most convincing people on the planet, revealing what they did and how to apply their strategies to your own life. Here are a few of the people we'll be introducing to you in the upcoming pages:

- The movie director who learned how to win over the toughest clients with his persuasive personality and become someone others admired
- The female go-getter who overcame extreme resistance in a male-dominated field to snag her dream job
- The technology startup leader who, after struggling to find his differentiator, boldly went after the top 1 percent of clients in his market and made his business a household word

Successes like these may be rooted in creativity, innovation, and hard work, but they can't happen without the ability to convince. We want to help you nurture that ability. If you're already pretty good at convincing, you'll learn some new skills. If you are just starting out, you will find your success grows much more quickly once you understand our strategies.

We believe that anyone, from a parent trying to get a recalcitrant four-year-old to go to bed to a startup entrepreneur angling for that first round of venture capital, can benefit from being more convincing. No matter where you are, the power to convince is yours to wield.

MOVE BEYOND THE NEGOTIATING SKILLS YOU'VE HAD SINCE YOU WERE FIVE

While you can improve your powers of persuasion, make no mistake: you had the basics down at age five. A 2020 study in the journal *Judgment and Decision Making* shows that by the time a child turns five, they instinctively "understand and incorporate supply and demand" when making a candy trade with other children.[1]

Additionally, the study showed that by age six, children are using advanced persuasion techniques such as "perceived value" and "self-interest" to decide how to divide up candy and cookies in a group. The most significant, world-changing negotiations in the history of mankind were based on the same seemingly innate principle of leveraging the other person's self-interest.

Unfortunately, many of us do not develop our convincing skills beyond the candy-trading stage. Convincing for grown-ups is more complicated. The situations life throws at us grow increasingly complex and require a more strategic approach. Effective convincing takes psychology, strategy, situational awareness, and yes, a slew of reproducible techniques you will learn in this book.

STOP RUNNING ON INTUITION—TELL YOUR GUT TO STAY OUT OF IT

Too many of us keep using the same intuitive approaches that have worked for us in the past, without modifying them to fit the situation or the individual. Convincing becomes an ingrained habit, performed by rote. Unfortunately, what worked before may or may not work now. Think of a boss who got his way as a child by sulking. Now he sulks to make his employees behave. It works with some, until they can find a new job. When it comes to persuading others, defaulting to their usual approach is precisely why so many people don't get what they want.

Every day, new experiences are shaping and changing your brain, a phenomenon known as neural plasticity. By turning off the convincing strategies you've had on autopilot since childhood, you can reprogram your brain, create new ways of thinking, and change how people react to you. In our pursuit to persuade others, we rely on rules of thumb that often turn out to be wildly wrong.

We will teach you how to adapt your convincing style to any person, in any situation. You will learn how to:

- Free yourself from the repetitive behaviors and negative self-perceptions that hold you back
- Push yourself beyond your gut instincts
- Read people and even entire rooms at a glance
- Use advanced convincing tactics that can dramatically improve your negotiation skills, your close rate, your career, and even your personal relationships

The book is divided into three parts. Part One, "The Art and Science of Convincing," provides an inside look at techniques and strategies that are effective in high-risk situations—and fully explains why they work from the standpoint of human psychology. Part Two, "How to Become an Expert Convincer," explains how to utilize these insights to develop your own convincing skills. And Part Three, "Applying Convincing Techniques to Your World," shows how to start utilizing your convincing skills in a variety of business, relationship, and everyday life situations.

Convincing isn't about making the strongest arguments. It starts with understanding the person you're trying to convince and their worldview. That's why we'll begin our journey with Chapter 1, where we will teach you the art and science of Forensic Listening. This skill alone will make you more convincing every day of your life.

PART ONE

THE ART AND SCIENCE OF CONVINCING

CHAPTER 1

THE ART OF FORENSIC LISTENING

When I (Chip) trained to become a hostage negotiator, I was taught an interrogation technique known as Active Listening. The goal of Active Listening is to de-escalate a disagreement and make the other person feel heard and understood in the moment.

While I had great success utilizing Active Listening as a hostage negotiator, I realized the technique had a significant limitation—it didn't provide a methodology to analyze the information people leave behind after the conversation is over. I felt I had to take the technique of Active Listening to the next level. To do that, I drew upon my previous career. Before joining the FBI, I served as pastor for two churches. As a minister, I guided families and individuals through life's most emotional events, from weddings to funerals. In transitioning from Rev. Massey to Agent Massey, I brought along a finely tuned sensitivity to human emotions. This ability to listen to and empathize with people in high-stakes, high-stress situations helped me understand the mindsets of hostage takers, spies, and violent felons as a hostage negotiator in the FBI's New York City Field Office.

FROM ACTIVE LISTENING TO FORENSIC LISTENING

By combining my approach with Adele's entrepreneurial skills, we created a technique anyone can use to better understand people. We call it Forensic Listening™. While Active Listening is done in the moment, Forensic Listening happens after the interaction is over (see Table 1.1). It is the art of reexamining what the other person said after they've said it, because words and behaviors leave clues. Forensic Listening is the art of finding and analyzing those clues. When and how people pause, what they emphasize, and what the tone of their voice communicates can be every bit as revealing as the words they use. By deconstructing these aspects of a conversation, the Forensic Listener can play back what was said to reveal a hidden narrative others may have missed.

Most of us don't have a dedicated listening strategy. We just focus on the words, nod our heads, and hope for a good outcome. We play it safe, using convincing strategies that have worked for us in the past. Then we wonder why we couldn't achieve the results we had hoped for.

TABLE 1.1 Active Listening Versus Forensic Listening

Active Listening	Forensic Listening
Purpose is de-escalation in the moment.	Purpose is to reexamine the conversation after it has happened.
Typically used in high-stress situations.	Effective in any type of situation to build a relationship.
Seeks to build rapport.	Seeks to build trust and penetrate hidden beliefs (i.e., their unstated narrative) over several conversations.
Technique has limited applications and rules of engagement.	A method used over time to uncover conversational clues (e.g., Targeted Validation, Predictive Statements, bringing them to better: future, self, and outcomes).

By mastering Forensic Listening, you will learn:

- How to tune in to someone so that they feel truly seen, heard, and understood
- How to respond with predictive statements that will bring out people's biggest fears, hopes, and dreams
- How to use these tactics to get at a person's Unstated Narrative—what they really want from this interaction, from you, and from life in general
- How to tap into that narrative to convince someone and, ultimately, get your way

A MOBSTER'S UNSTATED NARRATIVE

In my FBI days, I was sent to interrogate a drug cartel enforcer—let's call him Marco. Marco was in his early thirties and already serving multiple life sentences for eight murders, with no hope of being released. Knowing he would never leave prison, he had little incentive to talk.

My task was to get Marco's take on the operations of a rival drug cartel. There was no way to get the convict's well-deserved prison sentence reduced, so I tried other incentives—things like getting Marco a better cell, moving him to a prison closer to his family, or helping relatives of his who were already in the prison system. None of these options worked. Marco just stared blankly into the distance with a bored look on his face. Finally, I tried a different convincing tactic: getting to Marco's unstated narrative.

Before the next interrogation session, I researched Marco's criminal career by listening to tapes and reviewing informant interviews. While Marco was a man of few words, when he did speak, he was meticulous in his word choice and seemed to demonstrate a great deal of business acumen. He helped decide who was to be eliminated by managing a portfolio of risk. He measured risk for the criminal enterprise, risk of getting caught, and risk of being targeted himself. He also analyzed the potential upside. Year after year, Marco's analysis resulted in multimillion-dollar gains for the cartel. Marco was a businessman, albeit a murderous one.

Once I concluded that Marco saw himself as a successful businessman, I adjusted my interrogation tactic to fit Marco's self-image. "Marco," I began, "We're stuck. We could really use your insight. We're here because we're investigating another cartel, and we think you could help us better understand their operations and how these guys think. We've studied how you moved and the people you targeted and eliminated. I can't say that I approve, but your actions made good business sense. I must admit you were great at your job. Do you have any thoughts on what's happening with this other crew? What's my team missing?"

That's when Marco finally met my gaze. He offered up information on the rival cartel's possible next moves and motivations. I had identified Marco's unstated narrative—he wanted to be seen as an accomplished businessperson and earn the respect and admiration of his peers. Marco's knowledge was his legacy, vitally important to his self-esteem and the image he wanted to project.

If Forensic Listening can uncover the hidden motivations of a mob assassin with no hope for parole, just think what applying these methods to business and personal conversations could achieve for you! Everyone you interact with has an inner life rich with unstated aspirations and narratives that you can uncover through targeted questions and deep listening. And once you discover a person's motivations, you can negotiate the deal you want, one that works for both parties.

HOW TO FORENSICALLY LISTEN AT WORK

While business problems may not equal the high-stakes situations of true crime stories, they can feel every bit as stressful. Forensic Listening, as described in the hostage situation and the cartel interrogation earlier in the chapter, is the art and science of reexamining conversations after they've occurred. This process can help you become instantly more persuasive—giving you the power to better understand your own emotions and those of others.

One of our clients—let's call her Kristen—was a successful, smart, and capable professional, but the sharp edges of her personality were getting in the way of her promotion to senior vice president. While she was known as someone who "got things done," she often rubbed people the wrong way. Kristen's boss told her she would have to change her communication style before she could be considered for a promotion. When Kristen called us, she sounded defeated and defensive. She couldn't understand what she was doing wrong or how to fix it. It was clear Kristen would benefit from Forensic Listening. We asked her if she'd be willing to change the way she was listening in the meetings at work.

When she agreed, we gave her a step-by-step overview of our process:

1. Situational awareness
2. Emotional patterns
3. The power of understanding
4. Targeted validation

Situational Awareness

The first step in Forensic Listening is situational awareness. In law enforcement, situational awareness is the study of real-time threats and how things will likely unfold in hostile situations. In corporate America, situational awareness is about being able to listen to others, identify potential problems, and examine how they may affect us as well as the organization. Threats can be as simple as being marginalized in a meeting, managing a difficult boss, or dealing with an angry customer. To address these types of business issues, you must first study conversations and interactions with others in a specific way, such as examining:

- Emotional patterns that can change the pitch, tone, and cadence of their voice when they speak to you, as opposed to others

- Stories or themes they consistently highlight or return to
- How they want to be praised and what they praise in others

These three things will also tell you how they are going to deal with conflict. When a client of ours opened up about a difficult situation with his board, you could tell he was disappointed by how they criticized his decision. The pitch, tone, and cadence of his voice changed while describing the incident. Additionally, he kept pointing out all the things he did right during his tenure and repeating three major wins. Moreover, he described how he wanted the board to perceive his mistake, noting, "They could have been more forgiving, given all I've done for the organization, but they were ruthless in their criticism of me."

This process of examining a person's emotional patterns, the stories they tell, and how they wish to be praised (as well as what they praise) will give you a quick glimpse into their possible motivations.

Emotional Patterns

Perhaps of all the things to review mentioned previously, the emotional patterns are the most telling. Look for fear, anger, sadness, happiness, or any combination of these. How does the individual react to stress? When and how do they present these emotions? This is the first step in establishing a baseline of who they are and how to interact with them most effectively.

Additionally, you must consider your own possible limiting and/or self-sabotaging behaviors. That means maintaining a grip on your emotions! Be mindful of your facial expressions when you hear a bad idea. Try not to come across as listening for holes in an argument as opposed to finding opportunities to build on good ideas. Also, be cognizant of when you are being scrutinized, such as after a difficult meeting or when the pressure is on. This is when people are typically looking to make judgments about who you are and how you handle difficult people.

The Power of Understanding

The success of your interactions is directly correlated to your ability to understand others. That starts with creating a sense of safety and trust rather than coercion. Rarely is there a direct match between how someone feels about you (the tape running in their head) and what they express in words, body positioning, or even actions.

Forensic Listening will allow you to ask robust questions that help you build trust by making people feel respected and understood. One example is to cite a detail from a previous conversation. For example, you might say something like: "I remember you said you like to read *Harvard Business Journal* articles about workplace culture. I know that is something you are passionate about and thought you might like to read this new piece that came out today." This shows you listened, you remembered what was said, and you took something from it that was valuable.

Using Forensic Listening, you can recognize patterns of human behavior that move you to understand possible causation and responses. You will also be able to pick up on the signs of pushback before it happens and understand dysfunctional group dynamics so you can work around them. This power of understanding will give you the ability to move people to the desired outcome without making them feel cornered or manipulated.

Targeted Validation

The second step in Forensic Listening is to use the information you gathered in your initial assessment to target and validate the person you are trying to influence. Targeted validation is when you are listening for a specific area where you want to hit them with validation. It is a smart, quick way to build rapport and get others to see you as someone who thinks of them in a positive way.

How to Use Targeted Validation

What you want to do is show someone the importance and the legitimacy of what they've said to you. It's one thing to validate somebody, but we're talking about finding a very specific area to validate. So how do you identify that area? You want to identify the area where they have the most energy. It is what they like and what they value. You want to validate what they believe is the most important thing to them. Let's look at an example of Targeted Validation Adele used in her own home:

My son Christian is eight years old, and I got a report from his teacher that he had a behavior problem in school. Like any second grader, Christian has some very good days and some very bad days. That's just the nature of being eight. So I told my son, "Hey, listen, Christian, I understand you had a really bad day yesterday. Let's talk about that. And he said, 'You know, Mom, I had a really good day today. I think we should talk about that.'"

This conversation made me come to a few inevitable conclusions: The first thing is I'm raising a lawyer. My son possesses some serious convincing skills. And it made me think we may have something to learn from other second graders in general.

Second, I realized the most effective thing I could do was to practice Targeted Validation. And by saying, "Well, Christian, tell me about your day today then." And he did. Then I said, "Well, that's great. You should definitely have more days like today and not so many like yesterday."

Perhaps most important, Targeted Validation must be genuine, so be sure to pick the things you truly admire about them and what they said—even if those things are difficult to identify. Focus on traits or behaviors that can help you get closer to your goals. For example, you might say, "I noticed how you wouldn't let that client walk all over Andrew in that meeting. That was really smart, and I know it made a big impact on him."

The Importance of Belief

People need to feel believed to be motivated to take action. You can't discount someone's problem and expect them to be highly motivated to work with you to solve yours. In other words, you have to listen to people's complaints, valid or not, before they are willing to accept your truth.

When people see it's obvious you are working toward the advancement of their goal, they start to see you as an integral part of their success. Simply acknowledging that someone is taking on a challenging task shows that you respect the effort and understand the goal. This will demonstrate that you are on their side and want to help them get what they want. They will put you into their inner circle, or you can add them to yours. This combo of authority and belief is intoxicating and almost impossible to resist.

Forensic Listening Checklist

For this to become second nature, you must examine these seven things:

1. Look at what the other person is saying right now. Read signals, including their body positioning, posture, where in the room they choose to sit, and so on.
2. What emotions are they displaying? Are they anxious, excited, nervous, fearful, dejected, or angry?
3. What are you hearing in their voice—pitch, tone, cadence?
4. What themes do they seem to be repeating?
5. Is their behavior evolving during the interaction—are they getting irritated or bored? Do they sound complacent? Are they growing more enthusiastic?
6. Are they focused on blaming others, or are they solutions-oriented?
7. Are they seeking to bring in other ideas or just repeating their own thoughts?

KRISTEN'S STORY

Now let's return to Kristen, the competent but abrasive executive angling for a promotion. In fine-tuning her situational awareness, Kristen realized that she was so single-mindedly focused on her task list, she neglected to address her boss's questions and concerns around those tasks. When he gave her an assignment, she would frequently push back in front of others and give reasons why the project might fail. While she was often correct in her evaluation, her criticism was neither constructive nor diplomatic. She'd often say things like: "This is a really bad idea—it just won't work." Kristen was great at thinking fast, but she needed to develop a filter to slow down her responses. People saw her as an argumentative doer—not a collaborative leader.

We coached Kristen to use Targeted Validation and emphasize positive behaviors in others to help further her goals. When she was given a project she had issues with, she began by validating the end goal of the assignment. She took time to analyze the assignment and craft a response outlining her issues. Instead of immediately giving in to her need to be right, she demonstrated her expertise in a thoughtful, nonconfrontational way.

Kristen also began reviewing conversations in greater depth, assessing not only what people said, but why they said it. She turned out to be as quick at picking up patterns as she had been to voice criticism, and the Forensic Listening techniques we taught her soon became second nature. That's when things started to turn around. People on Kristen's team began seeing her as someone they could trust. Some even started coming to her for advice. Gradually, she built strong bonds with a few key people on her team. She asked the right questions, at the right time, and in the right place. In meetings, she even began using more advanced techniques such as Predictive Statements, a technique we will teach you more about later in the book. In a meeting, she was asked how to price a project for a difficult client. Her answer displayed her new skills:

> Given my experience working with this type of customer, I've noticed they tend to be conservative when creating a budget but understand they must boldly invest when the project is a high priority to leadership. With a company of this size, my guess is the spend for this product or service is somewhere between $60,000 and $90,000. Am I close?

Using Forensic Listening, Kristen was able to look back at her interactions with this customer and notice clear patterns of behavior. By adding "Am I close?" at the end of the question, she softened her answer so as not to seem like a know-it-all and implicitly deferred to her boss and other senior people in the room. Within six months of making these small, but significant, changes, Kristen was promoted to senior vice president.

This technique will work for all kinds of people, from all industries. Executives in some of the most respected brands are using this formula to increase sales, employee engagement, and innovation.

For instance, Fortune 500 companies like Deutsche Bank, Samsung, and SAP are teaching our methodology to teams all around the world. Facebook, now Meta, used it to change negative perceptions of their 2.89 billion active users. A small business used our methodology to go from $195,000 in sales per year to $1.2 million in just under nine months. There's no doubt that after reading this book people will gain confidence and courage to go after their biggest goals without hesitation or self-doubt.

The techniques you will learn in *Convince Me* are not intended to control or manipulate people. Rather, they are ways to better understand others and tap into the levers that motivate them. It's a power that comes from being observant, open, empathetic, and genuine.

If you use these convincing tools effectively, most people will reveal more about themselves. You'll start to understand their unstated narrative; what drives, motivates, and encourages them; and conversely, what frightens or turns them off. You'll be able to tailor your statements and questions to make your clients, colleagues, and bosses more receptive to your ideas, attentive to your concerns, and agreeable to your terms.

As you read colorful case studies from Chip's FBI days, you will learn how the techniques of a master hostage negotiator can be used to make everyday conversations, interactions, and situations go your way.

I will also share stories from my life in the trenches as a publicist and crisis consultant. My experiences may be less colorful and cinematic than Chip's, but the survival of businesses, careers, and professional reputations are, in their own way, also matters of life and death. We will explain the difference between grasping for a solution while in a state of panic and making the right decision swiftly, with a focused sense of urgency.

We will discuss how being open, genuine, and even vulnerable can help you get through to a skeptical prospect and make the sale or close the deal. We will share leadership techniques that top executives can deploy to build trust and inspire unity in difficult times. As you absorb and learn to use our convincing tactics, you will discover that they are applicable to a broad swath of interactions, across every aspect of life.

KEY TAKEAWAYS

- Active Listening is a technique for de-escalating disagreement and making the other person feel heard.
- Forensic Listening is the art of reexamining what the other person said after they've said it. While words leave clues, Forensic Listening also considers how the words were said in order to discern the other person's unstated narrative.
- Our step-by-step process to master Forensic Listening includes developing situational awareness, recognizing emotional patterns, building a deeper understanding of the person you're interacting with, and using Targeted Validation.
- By employing Forensic Listening, you'll discern people's unstated narratives; what drives, motivates, and encourages them; and conversely, what frightens or turns them off. You'll be able to tailor your statements and questions to make people more receptive to your ideas, attentive to your concerns, and agreeable to your terms.

CHAPTER 2

FINDING THE UNSTATED NARRATIVE

As a newbie special agent, I was starting a rotation with the FBI Fugitive Task Force. The DC field office had paired me with US Marshall Justin Vickers, a very experienced law enforcement officer. We were tasked with running down leads on the whereabouts of several fugitives, and Justin shared his MO for working these cases. First, you research all potential leads and identify addresses of people connected to the fugitive. Whether the lead is interviewed or surveilled depends on the fugitive's past and how long they have been on the loose, or as the FBI puts it, "in the wind."

When we got to our first stop, a Washington, DC, brownstone, Justin suggested I do the interview. We believed the house belonged to the subject's grandmother. "You know all the questions to ask," Justin reassured me. "We'll go up there together and we see what we find out about the fugitive."

As we approached the door, I remember Justin saying, "Don't knock too loud or too many times. That sounds alarming. Let's just wait and see if she answers." I was eager and a little nervous: I wanted to impress Justin. The door opened immediately, as though the woman was anticipating our arrival.

I did the official greeting. "Good morning, Ma'am. I'm sorry to bother you so early in the morning. My name is Special Agent Massey. This is US Marshall Vickers. Are you Mrs. Willington?" She nodded. "Jonathan is your grandson?" "Yes," she replied.

I started the questioning, notebook in hand. Justin stood behind me, observing the exchange. I had plenty of questions for Grandma:

> "When was the last time you heard from Jonathan? Was it by phone? Was it in person?"
>
> "I don't remember," she replied.
>
> "Did he say where he was staying or living?"
>
> "I am not sure."
>
> "Could he be with a girlfriend?"
>
> "I don't think so."
>
> "Does he have any friends or relatives in the area we could talk to?
>
> "I don't know."
>
> "Did he say whether he had found work anywhere?"
>
> "Can't say."
>
> "What kind of vehicle is he driving? Does it belong to someone else?"
>
> "I just don't know."

Clearly, I was getting nowhere. My exhaustive list of questions had yielded zero results. I ended as we always did. "We are going to give you our cards. If you hear from him, or any news about him, please give us a call. It's important."

She shook her head in agreement. I said to Justin, "Do you have any questions?" He just smiled, nodded no, and thanked the woman for her time.

While we were walking back to the car, Justin pulled out his cell phone and started furiously texting.

"Well," I remarked, "Guess that didn't help much."

Justin looked up.

"Hold on, Chip, let me finish sending this out to the team."

"Should we visit anyone else on the list?" I asked.

"No," Justin replied. "He's here."

"Come again?" I exclaimed. "How do you know he's there?"

That's when Justin gave me a quick course in body positioning.

"Did you see the way she was standing?"

I hadn't been paying attention because I was too intent on covering my list of questions to notice what has happening right in front of me.

"She was guarding the door with her whole body." Justin explained.

"Chip, that door closed a little more with every question you asked. This was a clear sign that she didn't want us to see what was on the other side. She wanted the encounter to end immediately. Did you notice she didn't ask if her grandson was OK? Or why we were there in the first place? You know why? Because she already knew."

After the backup team arrived, we approached the brownstone again. The suspect's grandmother answered the door immediately, like she'd been waiting for us to return. Her voice was very soft and faint as though she wanted us to bring our voices down so as not to wake somebody up. This time, Justin asked the questions. He spoke slowly and softly, his voice pitched low.

"Don't say anything," Justin warned the woman. "Just nod your head yes or no. He's here, right?"

She nodded, yes.

He then asked if her grandson was on this floor or perhaps upstairs. She nodded no to both. Was he in the basement? The woman nodded yes.

"Is he awake?" Justin inquired.

The woman shrugged her shoulders and nodded no.

Justin probed further, "Is he armed?"

She nodded, yes.

We summoned the backup team, entered the home, and arrested our fugitive.

WHAT DID I MISS—AND WHY?

Later, when he debriefed me, Justin went over what I should have noticed. First, the grandmother's positioning. Then her lack of emotion. "Did you see how hard she was trying not to seem scared? It just felt off," Justin explained. Another important red flag was the fact that she didn't ask about her grandson's well-being. In addition, the woman's answers were as brief as she could make them—also a strong indicator something was amiss.

How could I not have seen what my more seasoned partner saw so clearly that day? Intent on making a good impression on Justin, I was too focused on asking the right questions and writing down every detail to see what was right in front of me.

FORENSIC NOTE-TAKING: PUTTING YOUR POWERS OF OBSERVATION TO WORK

Imagine yourself in a meeting with your boss, a few colleagues, and a potential business prospect. Now, resist the temptation to check your phone, think about lunch, or simply zone out, and put your powers of observation to work. That means:

1. Listening with your eyes and ears, and not just your intellect
2. Taking notes in a new way we call Forensic Note-Taking (Figure 2.1)

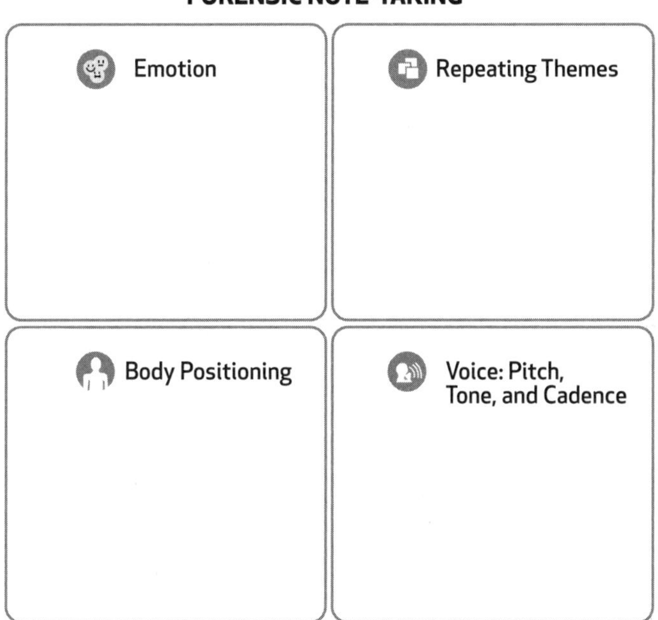

FIGURE 2.1 Forensic note-taking.

Forensic Note-Taking is a supercharged way of taking notes that can give you the insight you need to make an impact. Instead of just jotting down the content of what was said, you supplement that with observations about *how* it was said. It's a strategy that can give you a competitive advantage over others who are just taking notes to recall the conversation. (Obviously, you need to be subtle. Writing that "So and so is a jackass" is not the best idea. If you have illegible handwriting, you may find this to be a plus for the first time in your life.)

Forensic Note-Taking will help you decipher the tone of the people in the room. Remember how insightful Justin was about our perp's grandmother's demeanor? That's because he was paying attention to these four important aspects of her behavior:

- **Emotions.** How does the person you're observing feel? Do they appear empowered? Disengaged? Frightened? Excited? Dejected?
- **Themes and word choice.** What stories or words do they repeat or return to during the conversation? Do they sound like they are parroting someone else? Are they telling their audience what they want to hear? Repeating scripted talking points? Theme development in conversations will tell you what is important to the person sharing. What does their word choice reveal about what they are thinking?
- **Body positioning.** How is the person positioned relative to you or to others in the room? How do they shift their body when you talk to them? Is their body positioning open or closed? Are they actively looking around, or are they focused on the conversation at hand?
- **Voice: pitch, tone, and cadence.** People have individual verbal patterns when they talk, and these can reveal a

lot. Does the pitch of their voice go up or down? Does their tone change? Is their speech rapid? Careful? Halting?

All of this is important to include when you are taking forensic notes. Review the following exercise. It will help you become more observant and ultimately make you a more convincing communicator. You can do this in any type of business meeting, whether you are participating, presenting, selling, interviewing, or being interviewed. During the meeting, subtly jot down your behavioral observations along with your content notes. If you are in a situation where you can't really take notes, such as when you are the main presenter, take a few minutes after the meeting to write up your impressions. Then break out what you saw and heard according to the following categories.

EXERCISE 2.1: FORENSIC NOTE-TAKING

EMOTIONS

- What is the balance of power in the room? How are people responding to you? To each other?
- What kind of reactions do your words elicit?
- Do you sense tension? Boredom? Fear? Stress? Irritation?
- Is there a definite alpha person in the group?
- Do the others resent or appreciate their leadership?

THEMES AND WORD CHOICE

- Are there themes or ideas about the project your boss, or client, or another person in the room keeps returning to?
- Is there an elephant in the room that everyone is avoiding?
- Does a participant's communication style strike you as humorless? Dramatic? Understated?
  Do they use a lot of marketing buzzwords to show how on trend they are or mask the fact that they have nothing significant to say?

BODY POSITIONING

- How are people sitting? Is someone in a defensive, closed position, or sprawled on their chair taking up extra space?
- How does the person you are talking to adjust their body position as you make your pitch?

VOICE: PITCH, TONE, AND CADENCE

- Does the pitch, tone, or cadence of their voice change when you present an idea?
- What about when they have the floor?
- Does their voice tighten? Are they loud? Or very soft-spoken?

Your listener's emotions, themes, body positioning, and the pitch, tone, and cadence of their voice are clues to what they really think of your ideas. Looking for these types of cues will help you respond to people in an emotionally intelligent manner. It's strategic to monitor and manage people's feelings as deliberately as you do their mindset.

Once you have a baseline for what's at play emotionally, you can delve deeper to uncover someone's emotional motivators. These can be used as part of an advanced sales strategy to connect better to prospects and customers. People want to make sure their emotional needs will be met before they take a chance on a product, service, or idea you are selling. According to a study called *The New Science of Customer Emotions* 2015, some of the most common emotional drivers include:[1]

1. **Wanting to stand out from the crowd.** People want to feel like they are doing something unique and breakthrough, or that they themselves are one of a kind.
2. **Having confidence in the future.** Your prospect, boss, or coworker wants reassurance that your idea or offer will benefit them and their company.
3. **Enjoying a sense of well-being.** People want to feel their choices will help them maintain their health and peace of mind.
4. **Feeling a sense of excitement.** Depending on the circumstances, people may want to feel like their choices will lead to exciting outcomes.
5. **Experiencing a sense of belonging.** When people feel like they are part of something bigger than themselves, it creates a sense of emotional attachment and obligation.
6. **Being the person they want to be.** Aspirational thinking motivates people to reach for new goals. This can be an especially effective incentive.
7. **Feeling secure.** People want to feel the choices you are asking them to make will not lead to buyer's remorse.

Use these drivers to create a successful emotional sales strategy. For the best results, your pitch should connect to at least three out of seven of the emotional drivers listed previously. The more you can connect to those underlying emotions, the more convincing—and successful—you will be.

We were hired to consult with Community Brands, a large technology company that had just received an infusion of venture capital funding and was in a race to dominate its market. JP Guilbault, the company's then-CEO, knew getting people to switch systems would prove difficult, because at the time, everyone was using the same one. It was flawed, slow, and totally out of date, but switching technology providers would mean a tremendous amount of effort and extra work for potential customers and their staffs. To counter this valid concern, Community Brands' competitors minimized or even denied the difficulties of migrating to a new platform. The approach we recommended seemed counterintuitive: we advised Community Brands to acknowledge the challenges of switching platforms and use that as a sales and marketing tactic. Here's what they did.

Our advertisements for the platform included images of people doing difficult things, from wrestling a pig to white water rafting. The headline was, "Some things are messier than switching your technology." The ads explained that while the switch would be difficult, Community Brands specialized in making it as easy as possible for the prospect. This hit on a lot of the potential customer's emotional needs, including:

1. **Having confidence in the future.** Replacing and moving beyond the old technology would prepare the company for future success.
2. **Enjoying a sense of well-being.** The sales team made sure to mention how they would help reduce the strain

on an organization's employees by easing them through the implementation process. The impact of migrating to a new platform on stressed-out employees is something competitors didn't even acknowledge, much less address in a sales meeting, making Community Brands more empathetic to its customers' needs.

3. **Feeling secure.** Knowing that their employees' needs would be addressed made management less concerned about potential blowback and more comfortable that they were making the right decision in picking Community Brands.

Our campaign was so effective, prospects often mentioned it on their initial sales call, saying things like, "I saw your advertisement. You are the first technology company that gets what it takes to make this kind of a change."

Another example is our experience working with the sales team at a major defense contractor to come up with a sales strategy and messaging for combat drones. With a little digging, we learned that the sales team consisted of engineers who had never battle-tested any of the unmanned air vehicles (UAVs) they were selling to the US defense department. To help sell the systems, we assembled a team of retired, high-ranking Army and Air Force personnel to battle-test the equipment. The team was effective in connecting with the prospects' emotional drivers, by:

- **Inspiring confidence in the future.** The military will experience fewer casualties, win more battles, and so on. Even in the most difficult circumstances, this technology preserved the lives of soldiers and civilians in war-torn areas.

- **Attaching to a sense of belonging.** The UAV was designed to be used by the world's most elite soldiers. This equipment would also be tested out by a specialized group of soldiers handpicked for the assignment.
- **Motivating success.** As a soldier, knowing that a piece of technology will help you complete your mission successfully is critical.

After the messaging was switched to a more emotional pitch, the company's sales went up by 30 percent in one year. When you can make an emotional connection—and people are convinced—profits increase. According to a *Harvard Business Review* article, "Managing Emotions at Work," research shows that, for better or worse, "emotions influence commitment, creativity, decision-making, work quality—and you can see the effects on the bottom line."

Of course, people don't necessarily tell you what they are thinking and feeling. The only way to uncover it is to examine and study their Unstated Narrative.

THE UNSTATED NARRATIVE

The Unstated Narrative is the tape running through our heads in any given situation. This tape is based on our own ideas about who we are, who we want to be, and how we want to be perceived. There are countless Unstated Narratives covering every aspect of our lives, and each of us has accumulated quite a collection. Here are just a few examples:

- I must secure this project, or I may not get the promotion I need for my family to feel secure.

- I feel like my presentation is the best one—I know everyone else agrees.
- I hope no one notices how disorganized I am.

Your ability to convince someone is greatly enhanced if you can identify how they wish to be perceived and how they perceive you. Unfortunately, people don't tend to reveal this through their words or actions. It's your job to create a sense of safety to help them drop their guard so you can move them to a self-directed decision.

SUBTLE FBI APPROACHES THAT GET PEOPLE TO OPEN UP

We've all been there. You are sitting across from a new business associate, and you want to get a read on them, so you don't make a misstep. How do they see themselves? What do they want out of you? To get to the Unstated Narrative faster, you must practice Active Listening during the meeting, followed by Forensic Listening afterward. As you learned in Chapter 1, Active Listening is responding in the moment to reinforce an idea or de-escalate a potential conflict, while Forensic Listening is reexamining a conversation after it has happened.

One Active Listening technique uses Minimal Encouragers to keep someone talking, so you can get a better sense of what is important to them. Say things like, "Yes!" "That's right," "Correct," or the ubiquitous "a hundred percent." Affirmation makes people feel heard and can get them to reveal more about themselves.

To take this a step further, we recommend a Forensic Listening technique called the Maximum Compliment. This is when you compliment something someone said that was particularly effective during an interaction. This will ingratiate them to you. They will see you as someone who really listens, recognizes others, and is on their side—all of which should make them more open to your suggestions.

Situation: Discord with a Coworker

You had a falling out with a coworker because you received credit for something they came up with. They are bitter about it and are now often critical of your ideas in front of others. To combat this, use the Maximum Compliment. Next time you are in a meeting, praise something this person suggests and explain why you like the idea. Add in details to show you really paid attention to them, and watch them change their approach to you.

In Active Listening, use open-ended questions to help you get a sense of what they mean when they say something about themselves. Try questions like:

- "Can you unpack what you mean by that for me?"
- "Can you elaborate on your perspective?"
- "How do you feel about this now?"

These questions, which focus on emotional aspects of interactions, will offer people an opportunity to reveal things about themselves. Build on that using the Reach-Back™ technique, referencing something someone said in a previous conversation. This is a smart way to make someone feel heard by you, not just in the moment, but consistently. For instance, in the previous example described, you might say "Tyler, when you mentioned that new Corporate Social Responsibility initiative in our weekly meeting last month, it was something that stayed with me and influenced my decision to move forward with the CSR project."

Additionally, in Active Listening you label emotions. This is asking someone if they feel a certain way and waiting for their reply. For example, "You don't seem too happy about this, am I right?" This helps the person be present and gives them a sense of what emotions they are currently conveying. It also gives them an opportunity to correct the emotion if you have labeled it wrong.

In Forensic Listening, you are establishing a system for understanding how an emotion is being processed. This isn't about the moment it happens—it is about the aftereffects. Can you discover the purpose of the emotion? Is it a reaction? Or is it strategic? Will the person feel remorse after it occurs and admit why they were acting a certain way? Or will they act as though nothing happened?

MICRO AND MACRO BEHAVIORS AND PATTERN RECOGNITION

Let's say there is a blowup with your boss in a group meeting one afternoon. The boss is angry about the poor results of the latest customer satisfaction survey. You have seen this behavior before, but now you know how to practice Forensic Listening. You can now place these interactions into Forensic Note-Taking, which will allow you see what is happening with new eyes and give you the analytic tools to move in a positive direction for your team, your company, and/or your career.

Situation

You have witnessed this type of behavior from your boss before. Typically, he will come in the following morning, have a quick standing meeting with everyone, and apologize. He will make excuses, explaining that he is under a lot of pressure regarding these survey results and knows the front office is going to be very upset.

You have to look at your boss's behavior from a micro and macro viewpoint. First, let's examine macro:

- How does his behavior affect the team?
- Do they go hide in their cubicles? Send group texts all night complaining about their horrible boss and bad morale? Are they all polishing their résumés?
- Do they take out their frustrations on vendors and anyone else they can kick?
- How does this behavior affect the problem the boss was railing against?
- Do the boss's actions have any positive effects?
- Are people inspired to address the issues raised in the survey and begin executing on plans to move it to the positive side?
- Do the boss's actions compound the problem and further distance people from engaging with issues in a constructive manner?

Record your observations through Forensic Note-Taking, which will also help you determine behavioral patterns.

Emotional Pattern

What are the primary emotions your boss expresses when he is disappointed?

Themes and Word Choice Pattern

Are there themes or ideas about the project your boss mentions more than once?

Body Positioning Pattern

How does your boss's body position change or shift when you bring up solutions? Is his body position different when he addresses others?

Voice: Pitch, Tone, and Cadence Pattern

Does the pitch, tone, or cadence of his voice change when you mention the survey results?

Taking into account your boss's pattern of blowing up and then apologizing, ask yourself:

- What is your boss's mental and emotional state post apology? Could he be more receptive to new ideas?
- Does he welcome more candid feedback? Does he maintain a positive or upbeat attitude for a length of time? Is his behavior cyclical?
- What kind of interaction is he more inclined to welcome during this state?
- What types of actions or changes (if any) typically follow?
- Does he usually shutter himself away for a while before reemerging in a different mood?

Pattern Recognition

Let's say your analysis shows that after the apology, the boss likes to sit in his office with the door closed for a self-imposed time-out. When he finally emerges, he is in a much more positive frame of mind and can be heard making self-deprecating comments and laughing with others—until his next hissy fit. You have just documented a pattern of behavior that can help you identify when you could be most helpful (and influential) to your boss. You want to wait until right after the time-out part of the cycle to run an idea by him or ask for that raise or promotion.

As a result of using this system, you see the pattern emerge:

- When your boss is in his post-hibernation phase, he welcomes ideas and feedback like no other time.
- You also note that there is a window for this type of welcoming behavior.
- Usually by noon the next day, the overall surge of positivity is extinguished, and he has moved on to the next crisis.

Why is this important to know? You have identified a pattern and a cycle of behavior. More important, you now know when you can be most convincing with your boss. While everyone else is railing against him and his anger issues, you can take advantage of the calm after the storm to forge a better relationship with him and establish yourself as a trusted advisor.

Most people will not take the time to analyze the dynamics with their boss or clients in this way. More still would not seek to leverage his periods of good disposition and take the initiative to improve their own standing.

KEY TAKEAWAYS

- When interacting with a boss, colleague, or someone in your personal life, don't just listen to the words that are said. Focus on the person's emotions, themes and word choices, body positions, and the quality of their voice—a process we call Forensic Note-Taking.
- Strive to understand a person's emotional drivers. These may include wanting to stand out from the crowd; having confidence in the future; a sense of well-being; a sense of excitement; a sense of belonging; being the person they want to be; or feeling secure.
- Use Minimal Encouragers and Maximum Compliments to get people to open up to you and reveal their true thoughts and feelings.
- Study and learn to recognize a person's pattern of behavior so you can time important conversations.

CHAPTER 3

EFFECTIVE CONVINCING

If I could read somebody's mind as though I were watching a movie, it would let me become a main character in their story. Getting into someone's mind is exactly what is expected of hostage negotiators. From trying to understand what kind of person would take someone hostage in the first place to knowing what circumstances led them to that point—it is both an art and a science. Everyone has this ability, but hostage negotiators have honed it and practiced it in highly stressful situations.

FIVE STEPS TO GET INTO SOMEONE'S MIND

Here are five steps they use.

1. Set the Stage

Depending on the emotional state of the individual they are dealing with, one technique hostage negotiators use is to tell the hostage taker how the negotiation is going to work from start to finish. For instance, a hostage negotiator would say:

> Thank you very much for talking with me right now. I really appreciate it. I just want you to know that I want to talk about everything you are dealing with right now. I want to know what brought us here today. As we get to know each other, and you feel we can begin to trust each other, I want to make sure you are safe.

We call this setting the stage. Now that we have set the stage for you, let's hear from Chip.

> People often ask me, "How do you deal with the stress of being a hostage negotiator?" I was taught to dial in to the hostage taker in such a deep way that everything else fell away. All the noise of the squawking radios, flashing lights, helicopters overhead, news cameras, and a SWAT team at the ready completely disappeared.
>
> The challenge for me became what to focus on. If I am focused on the pressures and stress of the situation at hand, it can quickly degrade my ability to help the people who need it most. I could get lost in the idea of a gun on someone's head, a bomb that can go off at any second, or an angry kidnapper with a nefarious agenda. But if I get caught in this pattern of thought, all I will think about is how horribly wrong this situation could go. Then the stress could overwhelm me, and I could become part of the problem. This is true in business as

> well. It is your job to reverse the focus and concentrate on how you can solve the customer's problem.

2. Reverse the Focus

Chip continues:

> My job is to understand exactly what brought the hostage taker to this moment where their life and the lives of others are hanging in the balance. So I am reversing the focus from my own fears at that moment to understand what the hostage taker is going through.
>
> This has the effect of both reducing the pressure on the hostage taker and redirecting my own stress into helping them solve their problem. This will ensure my analytical brain is fully engaged and my hostage negotiation training will be most effective.

You can practice this in your personal and professional lives too. Let's say your supervisor calls you into her office, and she is livid about something she sees as your failure with a customer. While this is not a life-or-death hostage situation, your livelihood could depend on your reaction to her stress.

The first step is to focus on what your supervisor is experiencing from an emotional perspective (anger over a misstep, fear of her boss's negative perception of her leadership, pain from losing an account, embarrassment that she did not spot a potential problem early enough). All these things are at play. This type of negative encounter with an employer or client is likely going to produce a crisis alert in your brain.

Overcoming this feeling requires a mental shift from, "Oh my God, I am under attack. This is so unfair. I could lose my job," to, "This isn't an ideal situation, but I now have the tools to actually turn this situation around." While this person might still be in attack mode, you are reversing the focus. This will enable you to stay calm and analytical enough to solve the issue at hand.

3. Don't Be Defensive

The next step is to listen in a nonjudgmental way and not defend yourself. Your goal is to get your boss to tell you in as much detail as possible what happened and allow her to vent. Yes, even if it means enduring some off-the-chart criticism both professionally and personally. This is the same thing hostage negotiators do.

4. Apologize, Even If You Don't Mean It

One technique that works to de-escalate someone and gain the upper hand is apologizing as they are venting. Why? Because they will begin to move from focusing on what you did wrong to what the issue is at hand. When you remain calm while they go off, your analytical brain will become even more in control and focused. Your stress rapidly dissipates, and your perspective improves. The next thing to say becomes clearer. How to solve the problem comes to you easily. Before you know it, you are in complete control of how the conversation unfolds.

5. Convince Them There's a Better Way

Begin asking questions about what happened to get them upset, such as:

- What is the most important issue right now?
- What are you anticipating will happen if upper management hears about this misstep?
- How might we explain what happened?
- What are we going to do to fix it?

Each time you engage with your boss's emotional crisis, you are de-escalating yourself on a neurological level. You will begin to feel the weight shift from anxiety about your own situation to helping her. No longer are you battling the fear of being belittled and possibly even fired. Instead of worrying about defending yourself, you are now in a convincing mode.

Meanwhile, she is shifting her focus from why she is mad at you to what the two of you can do to fix the problem. These five steps will build your influence with your supervisor and firmly connect your analytical brains together, which you both desperately need to solve the problem.

IT'S NOT JUST A THEORY, IT'S NEUROSCIENCE

Your brain is discerning patterns as you interact with other people. Cooperating well together during a task creates something neuroscientists call "synchronicity." When your brain recognizes a pattern you've seen before, you neurologically sync with the other person, which increases mutual understanding, empathy, and cooperation.

"Synchronicity can be manufactured three different ways: playing games in small groups (six to eight people), storytelling, and mirroring each other's body language," according to University of Pennsylvania neuroscientist Dr. Michael Platt.[1]

As a simple example of syncing, Dr. Platt points to a study of professional soccer players. "When a player is trying to kick a ball into the goal, he must desync from the goalie in order to be able to successfully make the shot," Dr. Platt explains.

If the goalie is mentally synced with the player trying to score a point, he will anticipate where the next shot is coming from.

The goalie strives to remain synced with the player trying to score the goal. The player does his best to desync with the goalie and score that unexpected point. While desyncing is sometimes called for, business encounters most often use syncing.

Syncing has been studied in mice. Researcher Dr. Yevgenia Kozorovitskiy of Northwestern University put two mice in sync by zapping their brains with the same rapid frequency. Within minutes, any caution or animosity between the two mice disappeared. Suddenly, they were as inseparable as long-lost friends.[2]

When Kozorovitskiy's team repeated the experiment using a different frequency for each mouse, the mice did not display that sudden urge to bond. Humans are, of course, more complex creatures than mice. We can't run around zapping each other's brains to get what we want. We can, however, use our words and behavior to "zap" another person into feeling comfortable and heard when they are in our presence—in essence, to get them to sync with us.

Sync with the Other Person's Concerns

To convince someone in a business context, just like hostage negotiation, you must sync with their concerns. When you can immediately tie into what that person is experiencing during your encounter, you automatically become more relevant and relatable because "you get them." Translation: you are syncing. At the same time, just like the kicker trying to psyche out the goalie in Dr. Platt's metaphorical soccer game, you need to feel comfortable desyncing. This requires conviction.

How to Establish Better Connections

We can all agree syncing is hard to do in just one conversation or interaction with someone. That's why learning their behavior patterns using Forensic Listening will help you become better at relating to others. You will start to see things about those around you that weren't as obvious before.

Over time, if you practice gathering evidence from the people you are trying to relate to, you will find yourself having epiphanies about their behavior. You might think or say things like:

- "I never thought about their behavior that way before."
- "I thought this wasn't bothering them but clearly it was."
- "I thought this person didn't like me, but it was really (fill in the blank) ____________________________."

Once you figure out where this person is coming from, you might get triggered by their true intent. Their patterns of behavior may reveal things you won't like, such as you aren't likely to close the deal or you're probably not getting that promotion. It's important to keep your own emotions about this revelation in check. Instead, use this information as more evidence to build your case and develop a better relationship. Remember when you are helping to de-escalate an irate boss or customer or coworker, you are also de-escalating yourself.

Now you are thinking like a hostage negotiator. You ask yourself, What else might be causing the problem with this person? Is there more they have not stated overtly? After some digging, you might find out that something else is at play. Your supervisor may be upset because they found out your client changed their engagement in response to a recent board meeting. While it is extremely important to focus on what is vital to your boss at that precise moment, you must move your investigation into the circumstances affecting the boss's reactions. If you don't identify the true intent, you won't solve the real problem.

Provide Mitigation

Your value and influence grow and your stress diminishes when you can demonstrate an ability to keep calm and withstand slings and arrows. If you combine the ability to de-escalate with empathy, your power multiplies exponentially. By providing mitigation and not giving in to defensive postures and biting comments, your power will multiply even more. People will start to see you as an ally, trusted advisor, and storm-tested confidant. You weren't defensive. You apologized for the effect your actions had on them, and instead of storming off angrily to your cubicle, you made solid contributions to help them rectify the situation.

Congratulations! You just passed your first part of hostage negotiation training to be convincing in business. Now we want to delve into how to read people more effectively.

HOW TO READ PEOPLE AND WHY IT MATTERS

Reading people isn't just for secret spies, double agents, and former FBI hostage negotiators. The ability to read people and understand how they read you gives you a major advantage in every career and business interaction. Simon Sinek, the author of *Find Your Why*, said, "100% of customers are people. 100% of employees are people. If you don't understand people, you don't understand business . . . ."[3]

When you're able to accurately read someone, you're able to understand them on a much deeper level—which enhances your ability to convince them. You can use this power to get that high-ranking promotion, well-deserved public recognition, and bigger, more lucrative business opportunities.

What makes you interesting to others is your interest in them. It starts with understanding their Unstated Narrative—their vision of who they are and how they want to be perceived. This goes much deeper than an individual's title, salary, or education, all of which can be gleaned from a résumé. So how do you figure this out? Read on.

The 22-Second Reading: How to Read Others Effectively

Before working at the FBI, Chip was a Methodist minister. He has seen people through a variety of life-changing events, from getting married to losing a parent or a child. His knowledge of how people typically react in certain situations has taught him how to read people effectively. His experience in the FBI also gave him insight into how people act when they are under stress, being deceptive, or trying to manipulate others.

As a journalist turned crisis-management expert, I have learned how to assess situations quickly and make fast-paced determinations to advise some of the most powerful executives and heads of state. Perhaps my ability to do this easily can be attributed to growing up in an Italian American family in Long Island. I'm an empathetic straight shooter who can quickly assess other people's motives.

If you met Chip and Adele at a business function, you would see that we are just as approachable as anyone else. We tell stories, crack self-deprecating jokes, and have a good time. Meanwhile, we are simultaneously reading people. We use a technique called the 22-Second Reading, which describes the time it takes us to get a sense of someone's energy and persona. Perhaps one of the most overlooked tells, or revealing expressions, is this: Is the person we are meeting trying to connect with us or impress us? Are they thinking, "I really want to find out more about you?" Or "Gosh, I can't wait for you to hear about me." This will determine someone's level of openness to new ideas and fresh perspectives.

Many of you may be thinking, what about unconscious biases? Chip and I feel strongly that the idea of unconscious bias is corporate doublespeak and to put it plainly, bullshit. Of course, biases exist in all of us. That's just human nature. We are all sizing each other up all the time. To believe otherwise is not realistic. We are not telling you to be Machiavellian. We are simply suggesting you be observant in a way that furthers your goal.

If you were to listen in on our conversation after we meet a potential client or business associate, you'd see the system we are going to lay out for you play out in real time. Once you learn the Six Sides of an Interaction (see Figure 3.1), you will put this simple but incredibly effective process in place for yourself.

Your Style	Their Style
Your Story	Their Story
Your State	Their State

FIGURE 3.1 Six sides of an interaction.

So how do you master the interaction? How do you take connecting with and influencing others from guesswork to guarantee? It comes down to six key things to look for. First, your style, story, and state, and then their style, story, and state.

THE INTERACTION

At the base of the interaction is the reason. What is the purpose of this meeting? Is this an initial conversation or an ongoing discussion? What is the balance of power? What is your end goal? What about the other party's end goal? Is the meeting in public or in private? Here's a peek into our process to set ourselves up for success when we meet a new client.

Your Style

Like it or not, we all judge someone based on appearance, consciously or subconsciously. So let's start with your physical appearance. Are people prejudging you because of your age? Your trendy or conservative personal style? Do you appear cocky, controlling, or condescending? Or disorganized, hesitant, and easily intimidated? Is your ego showing? Are your questions revealing insecurity, impatience, or lack of knowledge?

Your Story

This is what we call your Unstated Narrative, your role in the interaction, your feelings, spoken and unspoken, toward the person you are interacting with, and how you wish to be perceived by them. This is the disconnect between what people believe and what they say.

Your State

What mood are you in? Are you under pressure to get specific results from this interaction? Are you distracted by other matters, such as having a sick child at home or getting ready to go on vacation? Think about how your state is impacting your counterpart.

Their Style

Is their style of dress casual? Formal? Artsy and eccentric? What is their body positioning like during the interaction? Is their communication style tentative, probing, overly verbose, or precise and to the point? How do they conduct themselves? Do they go along to get along? Are they defensive? Funny? Conciliatory? Confrontational?

Their Story

This is their Unstated Narrative, their role in the interaction, their feelings toward you, and how they want you to perceive them. You may sense an affinity or hostility toward you. When you are speaking, do they appear skeptical, distrustful, or distracted? Are they asking relevant questions, playing gotcha, or performing for the benefit of a higher-up in the room?

Their State

Do they appear open or resistant to change? Are they guarded? Do they seem more interested in getting a read on what their colleagues think than in forming their own opinion? Do you sense fear or a lack of sincerity? Are they trying to read *you*, and if so, how do they perceive your mood?

To read people consistently and effectively, be willing to listen to what they believe in, and desire and value most. Whether you are negotiating a contract, trying to get a teenager to make good life choices, or persuading your spouse to buy a new car, understanding and being able to sympathize and empathize with someone's position gives you the ultimate influence.

KEY TAKEAWAYS

- The five steps that hostage negotiators use to defuse a situation can be applied to other types of interactions. The steps are set the stage; reverse the focus; don't be defensive; apologize, even if you don't mean it; and convince them there's a better way.
- When you combine the ability to de-escalate with empathy, your power multiplies exponentially. By providing mitigation and not giving in to defensive postures and biting comments, your power will multiply even more. People will start to see you as an ally, trusted advisor, and storm-tested confidant.
- 22-Second Reading is a technique we use to quickly gauge someone's energy and persona. Perhaps one of the most overlooked tells is this: Is the person we are meeting trying to connect with us or impress us?
- The Six Sides of an Interaction is a method for assessing a person you just met based on their style, story, and state and simultaneously predicting how they might react based on your style, story and state.

CHAPTER 4

THE EXACT STEPS TO START CONVINCING

In a few short hours we can hammer out a negotiation, make concessions, and come to a deal. By the time people get to the negotiating table, minds are already made up. The pros and cons of the deal have been explored. The other party's objections and demands have been anticipated. Potential concessions to reach a compromise have all been considered. Changing someone's mind is a lot more difficult than a formal negotiation. It can feel like a Herculean feat, but it's well worth the patience and discipline it takes to succeed.

Most of us lead the discussion with our most strongly held position—we play our best cards first. We're excited to share the epiphanies that led us to our new understanding, as if that were enough to get another person to adopt our beliefs. While reinforcing our own opinion this way is deeply satisfying to the ego, it never convinces anyone of anything.

Take my dad, Jack Gambardella, for instance—one of the least convincing people I have ever known. As a subway conductor in New York City, he would often get asked for directions. He was a charming man with very good intentions and a lousy sense of direction. My father would get so specific about the various landmarks people would see on their journey that he would distract them from the actual directions. They went from being lost in the city to lost in his narrative. I've always thought that somewhere on Long Island, some poor guy who got directions from my dad 17 years ago is still trying to find his way back to Brooklyn.

Like many of us, my dad used the tools in his persuasion toolbox—his New York stories and his considerable personal charm. He played what he thought were his best cards first, not necessarily the best for the situation at hand.

While Dad tended to get lost in the details, I have a friend who has the opposite problem—getting to the point too fast. We were having lunch together recently, and she was unhappy with her sandwich. She took a bite and immediately blurted out to the waiter, "This sandwich is gross." She didn't notice him rolling his eyes, but I did. My friend had cut to the chase to share her conclusion: her sandwich was lousy. Her blunt delivery made her opinion seem arbitrary, and the waiter was not convinced.

Instead, she could have said, "I come here a lot, but today the meal wasn't that good. Could you let the chef know?" In such cases, the chef usually comes out to speak to the customer, at which point my friend could have pointed out the dry turkey, moldy bread, or missing mayo. She might even have gotten a free lunch out of it, or at least a new sandwich. She played her cards too soon.

The same is true for hostage negotiating. It's very tempting to say, "You're done for—the only way out is for you to listen to me right now." As Chip can tell you, cutting to the chase could backfire spectacularly and result in somebody getting hurt—or worse. Instead, he would try to build a rapport, saying things like "Let's talk about what brought you here today."

"THE SAGA OF RIGHTEOUSNESS"

Make your most important point first and your chance for convincing is gone, along with your logical talking points and that elusive feeling of intellectual superiority. You've turned off the person you are trying to persuade. Their opinion is unchanged, and they may be more entrenched in their beliefs than ever.

This is what Dr. Robert Bontempo, a professor at Columbia University, calls, "the saga of our righteousness."[1] His advice? "First, avoid the temptation to give people the history of your intellectual development on a particular topic." In other words, keep your epiphanies to yourself.

"Secondly," Bontempo advises, "You have to have the discipline to withhold your point of view." This is so hard for most of us. We desperately want others to see what we see, and we have very little patience for their perspective. That's why convincing is best done over time, in a slow, scripted, methodical process. It must feel natural. People don't want to feel like they've been cajoled into a new way of thinking. They want to come to the new conclusion themselves.

Social scientists think of convincing as a continuum. Psychologist Muzafer Sherif, who originated social judgment theory in the early 1960s, created a horizontal model to illustrate this (see Figure 4.1). The model starts with the letters A, B, and C, statements your counterpart is likely to agree with. Sherif called these the "latitude of agreement." The letters in the middle of the model, D, E, and F, represent statements that fall into the "latitude of noncommitment." These statements are neutral, with no positive or negative associations attached to them. The last three letters on the model, G, H, and I, are likely to be met with the most resistance, which is why they are in the "latitude of rejection."

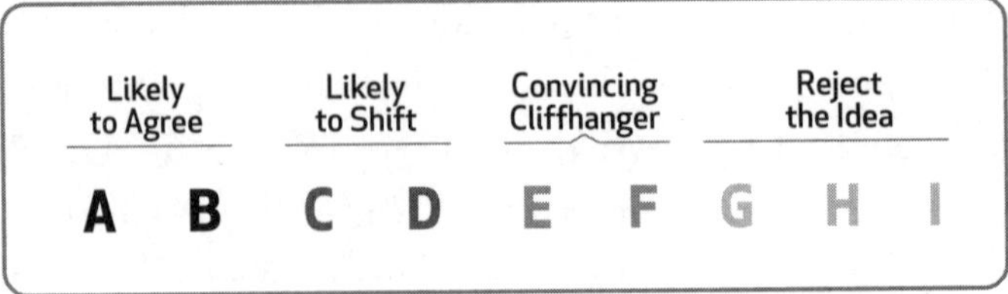

FIGURE 4.1 Convincing continuum.

Each letter on the continuum represents a series of statements that can be used during the process of persuasion. The science shows that the only information that changes anyone's mind is on the edge of the latitude of agreement, located between letters C and D on the continuum.

"If I go too far down the continuum to ideas that fall into your latitude of rejection, my ideas will not be consonant with the feelings in your limbic system," Dr. Bontempo explains. (The limbic system is the part of the brain involved in our behavioral and emotional responses.) "Once your limbic system is engaged," he continues, "your brain will go on fire. You'll be so triggered by your own thoughts and feelings you will not be able to hear mine—even if they make perfect, logical sense."

One client we worked with was a nonprofit promoting the benefit of internships. When they talked about their program, they liked to lead with the cost because they felt their offering was worth much more than the $10,000 program fee. While this strategy may have worked for them in prosperous times, they kept it going during an economic downturn and ended up in the crosshairs of an investigative reporter at the *Washington Post*. The reporter was investigating how interns were being taken advantage of and paying to work for free.

The nonprofit came to us for advice on how to deal with the situation. We asked them several questions about the benefits of the program and the pitfalls for students setting up an internship on their own. It turns out that without proper vetting and an organization to back them, interns who get their own placements are often not given real, meaningful work experience. They leave the internship with little to no experience that can be translated to the workplace.

Here's how we mapped out our client's message on the Convincing Continuum:

> **Statement A.** Our organization provides professional experiences that transform students' lives. We believe a structured internship, with learning at its core, should be available to all students at all income levels.
>
> **Statement B.** Sharon from Iowa State would never have been able to gain access to an opportunity on Capitol Hill without the help of our nonprofit.
>
> **Statement C.** After the internship was complete, Sharon used it as a stepping stone to get her first full-time job after graduation.
>
> **Statement D.** The nonprofit provides financial aid in the form of scholarships to 92 percent of students who attend the program from participating universities.

This messaging technique, rooted in social science, worked, and our client was happy with how the newspaper reported the story.

When we interviewed Dr. Bontempo for our book, he tried this exercise with Chip, using gun control as an example. He said, "Guns make us safer." Chip recoiled. That statement is triggering for Chip because as a former law-enforcement officer, he believes that if everyone had a gun, more people would use them and put others in danger. That statement would fall into Chip's latitude of rejection or G, H, I. It is inconsistent with the facts as he knows them and not consonant with his limbic system.

To better start the convincing process on gun control, we recommend starting with statements that would likely fall into Chip's latitude of agreement, like: "America has more gun violence than other countries." Chip agreed with that statement. That lands on A, B, and C on the continuum. Based on the real-time feedback, Chip would likely agree with statement B as well: "America has more murders per capita than any other country." Now, here's where the brain chemistry comes into play. What 40 years of research tell us is that the only thing that will change Chip's mind (or anyone else's) is statement C: "Gun regulation seems like an overreach, but more needs to be done to stop people from obtaining guns illegally."

"It's a statement that is on the edge of what Chip is neurologically hardwired to agree with, but hasn't considered before," said Dr. Bontempo. "It does not create positive or negative emotions." This is the only point on the continuum where Chip's point of view is malleable. This one conversation did not change Chip's mind on the issue of guns, but it may have moved further down the continuum and made him more open to a perspective he had not considered. Chip's boundaries for being convinced are now widened and therefore more open.

You may have truth on your side, but persuasion does not hinge on what is true. It's about what the person you are trying to influence believes is true. This is a key factor in understanding how far to push people down the Convincing Continuum. If you don't know where they stand, try asking a few open-ended questions to find out:

- What do you think about what we just discussed?
- How do you feel about it?
- Why do you think other people feel this way?
- When do you think this will addressed/fixed?

Start from a place that is mutually advantageous. For instance, we were approached by the management of a mall in a major city that was experiencing an uptick in crime. The holiday season was coming up and consumers felt skittish about shopping there. Because the mall was between police stations, the problem was largely ignored by law enforcement, with each precinct assuming the other would respond. By the time our client contacted us, they had already gone to the mayor for help, to no avail. The mayor claimed there was nothing he could do.

We quickly assembled a coalition of concerned business owners who were being impacted by the lack of consumer foot traffic at or around the mall. We filmed each business owner as they voiced their concern for their business and livelihood. Then we sent the video to the mayor.

The messaging was on the Convincing Continuum:

Statement A. We can all agree that small business owners create jobs and opportunities in our city.

Statement B. Mr. Mayor, we need help addressing this issue or I may have to close shop.

Statement C. We need to address this urgent issue now. I fear for my safety and that of my customers. (This statement was accompanied by CTV footage of a crime that took place outside the mall.)

Statement D. We followed up with a letter stating that if we didn't hear back, we'd have to send the tape of the impassioned business owners to the local television news station.

The mayor knew it was mutually advantageous to pay attention to what the business owners had to say. This form of persuasion worked quickly because we demonstrated that this situation was a crisis requiring the mayor's immediate action. Within 24 hours of receipt, police presence increased and the crime spree came to an end. A crisis can move someone down the Convincing Continuum faster. (You will learn more about how to make a crisis work to your advantage in Chapter 12, "Convincing Tactics and Negotiation.")

Let's take two seemingly different organizations: Exxon Mobil and the United Nations. "Most people are not willing to hear what I believe about Exxon Mobil doing more for the developing world than the UN." Dr. Bontempo told us:

> I believe that Exxon Mobil has done much more for the desperately poor in Sub-Saharan Africa, than the United Nations does. . . . A paycheck is sustainable development. When you create jobs for a community and you bring the dignity of work, a steady paycheck, that can help build an infrastructure that transforms communities. Providing aid does not; it creates dependency. I would say that the United Nations is a net negative and Exxon is a net positive in the Sudan.

This statement for many people would be a G, H, or I in the latitude of rejection. "Most people are not ready to hear those statements and they will automatically put me in the category of, 'Oh, you are one of those guys. You are a fascist who just wants to hold onto your wealth,' I am in their latitude of rejection, and they are unwilling to hear anything else," Dr Bontempo said.

For maximum impact and convincing power, you must start in the latitude of agreement:

Statement A. "I am sincerely concerned about the economic well-being of the Sudan."

Statement B. "If we don't fix this issue, there will be economic instability and civil war."

Statement C. "It's a terrible problem and we have to help those people."

Now the person hearing the message is ready to hear a new point of view. The reason why this works is they are not ready to believe until they are convinced that someone is a sincere and decent person. Once that happens, the boundaries begin to shift, and now they are more receptive to consider ideas at D, E, and F of the Convincing Continuum. At that point, the idea is to push small supporting proof points, paying attention to feedback. If this is as far as they can go along with you in this conversation, you must stop. If you don't, you risk backtracking on your progress. Try again in a few days to move them down the continuum now that their beliefs are shifting in your favor.

THE CONVINCING CLIFFHANGER

Sometimes, the person you are trying to convince needs to be nudged along the continuum. That's when we use a technique we call the Convincing Cliffhanger. This is the introduction of a problem that is plausible and intriguing, and requires the person you are convincing to challenge their assumptions and seek more information.

The Convincing Cliffhanger introduces F.U.D., which stands for fear, uncertainty and doubt. The goal is to make the other people think "Maybe I don't know as much about this topic as I previously thought." The other person's certainty is one of the biggest obstacles to persuasion, so you gently bring up something they may not know and let them chew on it. Creating uncertainty causes people to seek new information, relaxing their resistance to new ideas. The desire to understand what occurred and form our own opinion about it is too tempting to resist.

Using F.U.D. in Business

We were working with a newly appointed CFO. His communications team wanted him to stay "on message" about a controversial issue that was getting negative press attention for the company. The team had a strategy to control the backlash, but the CFO didn't want to take their advice—or ours. He thought he had come up with more compelling messaging than anything the communications staff came up with. So we introduced F.U.D. We suggested filming his response and then playing it back to compare his message to the one developed by the internal team to see which came across better. When the CFO was asked to review the footage and critique himself, he realized he just might be wrong about how the media would interpret the issue. He literally changed his own mind.

This is a technique I've used in messaging. Prior to President Joe Biden being elected, his communications team at the Biden

Cancer Summit enlisted our agency to call attention to the need for more funding for cancer research, which was Biden's "moonshot goal." The campaign yielded 225 media placements on various online and traditional outlets, including the *Today Show*. The reason our approach was successful was we started in the A, B, and C part of the Convincing Continuum:

> **Statement A.** Who hasn't known someone who has had cancer?
>
> **Statement B.** The cost of cancer care is astronomical.
>
> **Statement C.** We can all agree that we desperately need to find a cure for cancer.

Now for the Convincing Cliffhanger: The Biden Cancer Initiative strives to reduce the rate of cancer in half in the next 25 years. We need a better healthcare system to accomplish this goal.

We had to stop there. President Biden was looking to communicate the need to strengthen Obamacare, a statement that most voters would place in the "latitude of rejection." Based on where America was after the Trump administration, we knew this was as far as we could take voters—so we stopped. This initiative raised awareness, inspired more discussion about cancer research, and rallied people around the universal hope for a cure. It was also pivotal in raising support for Biden's presidential run.

THE BRAIN ON CHANGE

Let's say you take someone down the Convincing Continuum, find the perfect cliffhanger, and are successful in bringing them along to your point of view. Research shows you must pass through three steps to make an impact in someone's mind. Here's what behavior change looks like in the brain

Step 1: Unfreeze Existing Cognitive Structure

This is what attitude change looks like in your brain. Figure 4.2 represents how your opinion is currently structured. This represents your existing beliefs reinforced by your values, upbringing, education, experience, and so on.

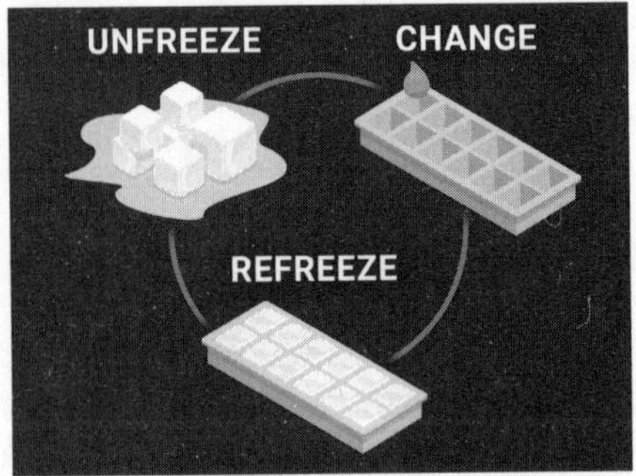

FIGURE 4.2 Lewin's change management model.

Step 2: Move

Once we understand a person's current cognitive structure, we must break their previously held beliefs by opening up their mind to new possibilities. This starts with getting them to see that you are a good, sincere person with positive intentions. Your goal is to get them to drop their defenses.

Step 3: Refreeze into New Cognitive Structure

Finally, you need to lead the other person to a new way of thinking and refreeze those beliefs in their mind.

A real-world example of this is the Eads Bridge story. The story illustrates that if you can't get people to believe in what you are talking about, you've got to find something they do believe in and then match it up to move them down the continuum.

Andrew Carnegie had spent a considerable fortune erecting the Eads Bridge. So on July 4, 1874, 300,000 people and a slew of reporters came out for an Independence Day parade commemorating the bridge in St. Louis. At this time in history, one in four wooden bridges collapsed under too much weight, so the public was very wary as they'd never seen a bridge like it before. It was the first steel bridge of its kind ever built, and it was also the only place a train could cross the Mississippi River. Getting people to cross it was another matter entirely.

In the 1800s, people believed an elephant would instinctively refuse to cross something that wouldn't support its weight. Knowing this, Carnegie thought, "If they had an elephant walk across the bridge, without hesitation it would prove to the public it must be safe for them too."[2] The fact that the bridge would have almost zero elephant traffic is irrelevant. The elephant is a perfect example of a Convincing Cliffhanger.

The Convincing Continuum is an overarching structure that can be generally applied to the convincing process. However, effective convincing must be customized to the person you are trying to sway. That's when you turn to more specific tools such as knowing someone's Unstated Narrative, using Forensic Listening, and understanding their Pattern of Life (POL) (defined in Chapter 9, "The Business Benefits of FBI Behavioral Analysis").

The right communication style can make these techniques even more effective. Keep returning to stories and internal themes that are important to the other person. Understand how they express themselves to determine what type of language to use when you are communicating with them. Are they blunt? Reticent? Overly composed? Gregarious? Do they respond to humor? Do they cringe if they hear a swear word? If people feel at ease with you as a person, they will be more open to your opinions, ideas, and ideals. They'll be more receptive to what you say and more apt to follow your lead.

Whatever your politics or opinions, you must remember that the process of changing anyone's mind about anything can be deeply threatening to them. What they think and feel is a big part of their identity.

THE FOUR STEPS TO USING THE CONVINCING CONTINUUM

Step 1. Show you are sincere, confident, and decent. People tend to believe others who share their values and opinions. If they don't perceive you as a "decent person" and they believe what you believe, they may question what that says about them.

Step 2. Use a script to carefully move people down the Convincing Continuum to your strongest point of view. Ideally, you will have at least three talking points and a Convincing Cliffhanger to represent the most important part of the continuum.

Step 3. Use F.U.D. (fear, uncertainty, and doubt). Remember, someone's certainty can be one of biggest barriers to convincing them.

Step 4. Create unresolved tension. Give the person you are persuading something to think about and ponder on their own after you've planted seeds of an important idea. You must leave them with a Convincing Cliffhanger to unfreeze the current cognitive structure of their beliefs.

KEY TAKEAWAYS

- Changing someone's mind is a lot more difficult than a formal negotiation. Starting off with your strongest point first is often a mistake because you're likely to turn off the person you are trying to persuade, leaving them even more entrenched in their position.
- Social scientists think of convincing as a continuum. Psychologist Muzafer Sherif created a horizontal model that starts with a latitude of agreement, which is an area of agreement between parties. The next phase, the latitude of noncommitment, is an area with no positive or negative associations attached by either party. The final phase, the latitude of rejection, reflects areas of disagreement. Moving carefully along this continuum is the most effective method to change someone's mind.
- We sometimes use what we call a Convincing Cliffhanger, which is a problem that is plausible and intriguing, and requires the person you are convincing to challenge their assumptions and seek more information. It's designed to unfreeze the cognitive structure of someone's beliefs by introducing fear, uncertainty, and doubt.

PART TWO

HOW TO BECOME AN EXPERT CONVINCER

CHAPTER 5

BE CONVINCING OR DIE "CONFIDENTLY" TRYING

Cajoling a coworker to pick up the slack on a group project.

Getting a five-year-old to eat her vegetables.

Selling a potential client on your company.

Not a day goes by when you don't have to convince someone of something. How confident are you in your convincing skills? In your abilities? In yourself?

In this chapter we will examine the role confidence plays in the art of convincing. You will see how coming off as either over- or under-confident can keep you from effectively selling yourself and your ideas. We will introduce you to several people who came tantalizingly close to convincing the world they were worth taking a chance on before succumbing to self-sabotage. And we will tell you how to avoid a similar fate.

THE OTHER SIDE OF HOPELESSNESS—THE CONFIDENCE TO CHANGE

Confidence is an empowering emotion. You're not confident in a vacuum: you're confident about something, whether it's your personal charm, your ability to lead, or how well prepared you are for tomorrow's presentation. Confidence implies that you are a dynamic person, someone who's on their way to ever greater success.

So why is it so hard for many of us to feel confident about our abilities? Why do we minimize our successes and fixate on our losses? Perhaps it is because the confidence to change is usually found on the other side of hopelessness. Do you describe your work environment using clichés like these?

- My back's against the wall
- There's no light at the end of the tunnel
- Dirty work
- Back to the drawing board
- The daily grind
- Another day, another dollar
- When you are going through hell, just keep going

Expressions like this signal deep dissatisfaction, or even hopelessness, about one's work situation. When hopelessness rears its ugly head in your professional or personal life, it's a signal that something must change, and not just your work situation. You need to change too.

Everyone, even the most successful people, has moments when they're running low on hope. Maybe you fell short on a goal, were passed up for a raise or promotion, or didn't get that new job you so desperately wanted. Perhaps you have convinced yourself that you're not reaching your true potential. If you get stuck in the quicksand of hopelessness and can't move past your fears, everything you desire will always feel slightly out of reach.

The First Person You Must Convince Is Yourself

"If you need to convince somebody of something, if your career or social success depends on persuasion, then the first person who needs to be convinced is yourself," said Professor William von Hippel, head of psychology at the University of Queensland.[1]

Convincing yourself is critical for your professional success. As a publicist who has gotten her clients in prestigious media outlets like the *New York Times* and on the *Today Show*, I can attest to this from personal experience. Before my clients score their first big media opportunity, they tend to be nervous and insecure. They may show signs of imposter syndrome and believe everyone else has something better to say than they do. As soon as they get that first big win, all that self-doubt dissipates. They can't wait to score new media appearances and wonder what opportunities they might have missed in the past.

We train our most successful clients to ride their own confidence wave after each win. They become unstoppable because they believe they deserve the media attention. They take full advantage of the fact that this is their moment to be recognized, noticed, and quoted. According to von Hippel, "We seem to intuitively understand that if we can get ourselves to believe something first, we'll be more effective at getting others to believe it."

Boosting Your Confidence

To give yourself the confidence you need to be more convincing, take a few minutes to examine what you excel in. Think about:

- Times when you were celebrated, awarded, or praised, or recognized for an accomplishment
- Skills in which you are naturally gifted
- Moments when your quick thinking or expert handling of a person or situation saved the day at work or in a life situation

Recount instances where you believed you were at your absolute best. Channel those moments when you felt powerful, unique, and downright unstoppable. Relive these experiences and bask in the glory of your wins. Feel like you're bragging? Don't. This is between you . . . and you. Cranking up your confidence will make you much more convincing, and the first person you need to convince is yourself.

Advice from a Hollywood Casting Director

During the writing of this book, Chip and I sat down with a well-known Hollywood casting director, Ellen Jacoby, to talk about how some would-be actors prepare for an important audition. "When people audition for a part," Jacoby said, "they must exude positive control over everything they do—power, presence, and status—and own it without hesitation. When the actor walks in, he or she must have already made a choice about what the character is about." Jacoby went on to explain that people who do best in auditions create a believable world for their character to live in. "Actors determine all the aspects of their character, including how to walk, talk, eat, and dress," she said. "They only fail when they get caught up in their own traps."[2]

You may not be auditioning for the lead in a movie, but you too can get caught in your own traps. The confidence to be convincing only comes when your intention and actions become the same. You must own your convincing abilities.

The Confidence Scale

While confidence is a powerful asset to help you be more convincing, there is such a thing as being overconfident. Psychiatrists refer to this as the overconfidence bias. University of Arizona Associate Professor of Marketing Martin Reimann does research on trust as it applies in business and marketing. In a recent paper, he wrote that, "People might wear a mask of overconfidence to try to appear more capable—a concept called impression management—but doing so can have the opposite effect."[3]

Projecting too much confidence can hurt you. People may see you as arrogant, conceited, or brash—all unflattering ways to describe someone who has taken confidence too far. The Confidence Scale has tipped too far in this case. Unfortunately, many people automatically think the opposite of overconfidence is humility. Many of us have been trained to view touting our own accomplishments as socially unacceptable. We are afraid to look like we are bragging. The truth is excessive modesty can be as much of a turnoff as cockiness. It can make you sound insecure and ineffective.

Vince Lombardi, arguably the greatest football coach of all time, is reported to have said, "Confidence is contagious. So is lack of confidence." If you come off as confident, your audience will have confidence in you. If you come off hesitant, your audience will hesitate to buy into your message.

Think of the Confidence Scale from 1 to 5. You want to be a 4 but not a 5, which will make you appear too cocky and impact your ability to convince people. This is a judgment call you must make for yourself, but your audience can help. Look for these signs that your message is being well-received:

- Excitement to speak with you during and after your presentation
- Mirroring of your emotions, body language, and the pitch, tone, and cadence of your voice
- Nodding assent and looking at you as opposed to their notes, their colleagues, or their cellphones
- Increased engagement as you discuss outcomes that are desirable for you as well as them—this means they are projecting themselves into your presentation

Somewhere between doormat and egomaniac, you will find that sweet spot that won't let others dismiss you as either cocky and overbearing, or wimpy and insecure. Let's look at some of the ways you can calibrate your confidence for the most effective convincing.

Be Confident, but Not at the Expense of Others

Professor Reimann's study shows that projecting confidence yields positive results, but only when it is noncomparative. Recognizing your own expertise and experience is fine if it's not at the expense of a colleague or competitor. You don't prove your competence by tearing others down.

Picture yourself in a presentation. The meeting is off to a good start when Matthew, your young, overeager colleague, goes in for the hard sell. He starts to talk about your company's capabilities. He provides noteworthy social proof in the form of case studies from happy clients. He shows off awards your company has achieved for the type of work your client is requesting. So far, so good. Then Matthew starts to bad-mouth the competition. "Our competitor doesn't have half of our credibility or experience in this space. In fact, they messed up a job for one of their clients who then hired us to fix it." The sale was lost the moment Matthew began slamming the competition. Confidence at the expense of others causes people to question your discretion. What might you say about them if the deal or the relationship doesn't go as planned?

I once represented a company that specialized in experiential gifts, such as biplane rides, kayaking adventures, and private race car lessons. I had secured a media placement on the front cover of the *Washington Post*'s holiday gift-guide section. (At the risk of being accused of overconfidence bias, I must admit the placement and the timing were perfect!) Both my client and the reporter were thrilled: my client had promised to take the reporter on a hot-air balloon ride as part of the interview. Unfortunately, during his first call with the reporter, my client went into full bragging mode. He listed all the reasons why his company was better than his competitors in the experience gift-giving space. Instead of doing the feature story she had promised my client before the interview, the reporter ended up writing a general article about his new field and mentioned all his competitors. My client couldn't understand why.

When my client and I had our postmortem, I said, "Mentioning your competitors' weakness in the space exposed problems within your business and made the reporter want to dig for more information. A better strategy would have been to expose a problem within your business and explain how you solved it and got better at what you do as a result."

In addition, the concept of experiential gifts was still relatively new. If my client hadn't mentioned his competition, the reporter might not have researched them. He wasted an opportunity to own his category in the business world. Instead of coming off as an innovator, he was mentioned as part of a new phenomenon, along with his competitors. Exposing your competition's weaknesses makes people question yours. Your biggest convincing obstacle is never your competitors: your obstacle is yourself.

A Touch of Self-Deprecation

Self-deprecation has a bad rap. Some argue that it lowers your credibility and has a negative impact on your self-esteem. If you indulge in self-deprecating humor, you may occasionally encounter some overly earnest (and possibly humorless) person who tells you not to put yourself down.

While you don't want to overdo it, a touch of self-deprecation can help you come across as more likable and authentic. If you're comfortable with occasionally making fun of yourself, here are a few things to keep in mind:

- **Choose a minor foible or flaw.** If you joke about finishing an entire bag of Oreos, folks will be amused. Confessing to downing a fifth of vodka in one sitting won't get you the same results.
- **Don't make fun of yourself for something you know you're good at.** It will come off as humble bragging rather than as having a little fun at your own expense. Nobody likes the model who calls herself "fat" for going up a dress size.
- **If you can use self-deprecation to flatter your audience, go for it.** For example, you could joke about

your passable computer skills to a technology company or wryly comment about your stubborn 10 pounds to a room full of personal trainers.

- **Don't use excessively negative language, like "I'm so stupid."** Instead, choose something softer, like "Silly me."
- **Be careful of overdoing it, especially if you are a woman.** Women tend to be very self-deprecating when kidding around with their friends. However, addressing a mixed audience of strangers is very different from dinner with your homegirls. Overdoing the self-deprecation can damage your credibility.

The Frank Technique

The Frank technique is a sales, marketing, and leadership tool that can benefit everyone in your organization, regardless of their position in the company.

We named this technique in honor of Frank Peters. Don't bother googling Frank. He's not famous. The odds that you would know him are remote, but you're about to learn why everyone who knew him loved having him around. A friend of Chip's older brother Mike, Frank was fascinated by planes and dreamed of becoming a pilot. Even as a teen, Frank was an incredible storyteller. One story has stuck with Chip all these years. He remembers this as though it were yesterday.

> One day, Frank began talking about ultra-light flying. He told me you don't need a pilot's license to operate this type of plane. You just put that baby together and take off! I was 14 years old, with no driver's license, much less a pilot's license, and I was captivated! "You

> know, Chip," Frank told me, "We could do this. We could be at the farm and build this ultra-light bird for you to fly it around in." I was astounded. This was something I could do? "Yeah, absolutely," Frank asserted. "You can do that." Now, I know what you're thinking: this whole thing sounds horrendously dangerous (it is) and I was a gullible teenager (up for debate). But this is the part I want you to focus on. Frank painted a picture of building and flying this ultra-light plane based on his own experiences. Then he did something especially powerful: he gave me a role in that story. He convinced me that, just like him, I could build this plane. He inspired me to visualize myself flying over the family farm. I was totally enthralled by the idea.

Most people tell stories about themselves. Frank hooked his listeners like rainbow trout, pulling them into his tales. He got people involved and kept their attention. That's what made him memorable, fun to be around, and very, very convincing. The Frank technique helps our clients—whether they be high-ranking executives, corporate employees, or ambitious entrepreneurs—get the results they want from their interactions.

Frank instinctively understood what the most influential people do to convince others. By casting your listener in your story—creating a role for them and an opportunity to relate and empathize—you are building a rapport with that person. They may not understand why, but they will remember you, your story, and how you made them feel. You have established a foundation for relationship you can build on in the future.

Share the Spotlight

When I was working on Madison Avenue in my mid-twenties, I scored a major media placement on the cover of *Time Magazine* for the CEO of 1-800-Flowers. I did this thanks to a media contact who also happened to be my former college roommate. This was my network, my win, and mine alone! I was proud of my big score, and it never occurred to me to share the spotlight with my team. Why this made me unpopular with my colleagues was beyond me. Then my boss, Zoe, said something I will never forget. "We all know it was your (media) hit," Zoe explained, "but by not sharing your success with others, you come off too cocky."

How could I have handled this better? Before I made my move, I could have taken several colleagues into my confidence, explaining that I had this contact who could help with the perfect placement. After the placement was made, I could have acknowledged someone else's contribution to the process. Strategies like these strengthen teams and make people feel included. People value feeling valuable.

Acknowledging people who contributed to your big win will help you garner bigger, better wins in the future. People will see you as a generous, trustworthy team player. They will be more likely to share information with you, bring you in on interesting projects, tell you about new opportunities, and give you a glowing recommendation when you need one.

KEY TAKEAWAYS

- Confidence plays a significant role in your ability to convince. Coming off as either over- or under-confident can keep you from effectively selling yourself and your ideas.
- Think of confidence on a scale from 1 on 5. You want to be a 4 but not a 5, which will make you appear too cocky and reduce your ability to convince people. This is a judgment call you must make for yourself, but pay attention to the reactions of your audience.
- While having confidence in yourself, your team, or your company is important, do not belittle your competitors in an effort to build up your side. It turns off your audience.
- Try using the Frank technique, which involves casting your listener in your story and giving them a role and an opportunity to relate and empathize. They may not understand why, but they will remember you, your story, and how you made them feel.

CHAPTER 6

WHAT THE MOST CONVINCING PEOPLE DO TO FORGE A LASTING BOND

We all have our own rituals to reduce tension. Meditation. A glass of wine. A quick run in the park. But tension, when it comes to convincing, can be extremely useful. Without it, you may not be able to persuade anyone of anything.

Too little stress results in complacency and procrastination. Too much stress raises our anxiety level to where it negatively impacts performance. Somewhere between those two extremes is a sweet spot for optimum performance. This is supported by research done in the early twentieth century by psychiatrists Robert Yerkes and John Dillingham Dodson.[1]

They developed a theory known as the Yerkes-Dodson law. The two were studying the relationship between stress and task performance. What they found is that there is an optimal level of stress, or arousal, at which we achieve peak performance (Figure 6.1).

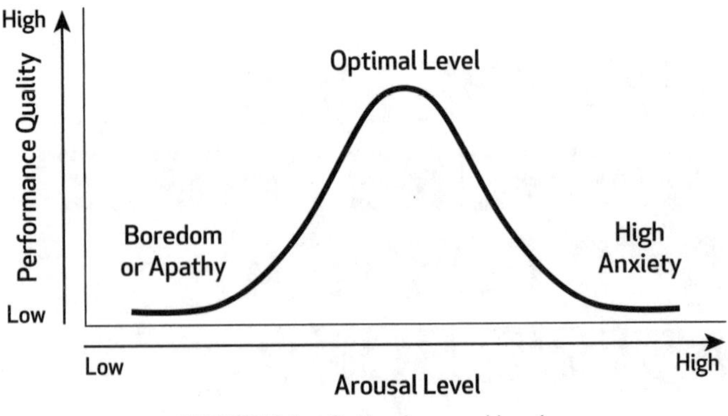

FIGURE 6.1 Optimal arousal level.

Harnessing the right amount of stress is both an art and a skill for leaders in today's business environment. Based on our experience working with some of the most convincing people in the world, much of what Yerkes and Dodson's research revealed holds true.

We developed our Convincing Curve based on the Yerkes-Dodson law. The idea is that there is a convincing sweet spot for both you and the person you are trying to influence. You need the right level of tension to communicate enthusiasm without being over the top. At the same time, you must raise the other party's tension level to engage them just enough, but not so much that they start to feel threatened, manipulated, or stressed out. As a leader, you tap into this form of tension to convince yourself or others in high-pressure situations. This is a powerful skill in a variety of common business situations such as:

- Motivating a lagging marketing or sales team without stressing them to the point of burnout
- Inspiring investors to buy into an idea without seeming overeager
- Asking your board to stand with you during a turbulent economy

THREE STEPS TO CALIBRATE EXCITEMENT

Effective convincers adjust their pitch to calibrate the other person's state of excitement. You can do this in three easy steps:

1. **Shake their confidence.** Raise the tension as you introduce the person to the solution you propose.
2. **Demonstrate how to change.** Show how your solution will help them grow and change in response to the conflict and circumstances they are facing.
3. **Insert maximum tension.** Tell them how you will solve their "biggest challenge." Usually, this is where you insert maximum tension.

I did this instinctively with one of my first clients, a cupcake shop. I started my first business, a boutique luxury PR agency, in 2008 at the height of the Great Recession. Can you say bad timing? I was going against the odds, but I was determined to make my business a success.

I was approached by two young women, first-time entrepreneurs, who wanted me to promote their fledgling cupcake business. Trouble was, there were already other several competitors with much deeper pockets making headlines, such as Magnolia Bakery in Manhattan. I decided to put the ladies through my "So What Test." This is the first step in sowing the seeds of tension. Here's how the conversation went:

Them: We left careers in finance and fashion to start this business.

Me: So what? The media doesn't care.

Them: Our cupcakes are delicious.

Me: So what? That's just what people expect.

Them: Our cupcakes are $4 each.

Me: That's a deterrent.

Them: We sell out every day.

Me: Now that is something I can work with.

As you can see, I shook their confidence a bit to create tension. Now that I had them primed, I implemented the second step. I demonstrated how my solution would use the circumstances they were facing to their advantage and help grow their business. Their original tiny storefront was located on a side street in Georgetown, an elite Washington, DC, neighborhood. I suggested pushing the countertop out closer to the door, creating a line outside the shop. This created, pardon the pun, instant word-of-mouth appeal.

Then I implemented the third step. I emphasized the challenge we faced in convincing the media to pay attention to the cupcakery, and hit them with my unorthodox solution: promoting the line! What I realized was that tastiness and snob appeal were not enough to sell people on the shop. But a cupcake other people were willing to wait in line for had to be something special. I used the Convincing Curve to sell the aspiring cupcake mavens on my strategy. We pitched the "cupcake line experience" to the media, specifically the famous *New York Times* food critic, Frank Bruni, and the business took off. More than a decade later, there's still a line outside that store.

RECIPROCITY AND THE ART OF CREATING CONNECTIONS

As we were writing this book, Chip and I discussed the process with our respective networks. We talked about our research, the people we interviewed, and the actual writing process. We even shared how hard it was to meet our deadline for turning in the manuscript. In the process, we were getting validation for the project and building support in our professional network.

Perhaps the most effective strategy to forge relationships and build your network is understanding what someone's true passion is and use that to drive connection. As a die-hard Elvis Presley fan, I wrote a post on LinkedIn detailing how the king of rock and roll was one of the greatest examples of good marketing and PR. I told the story of how, as an 11-year-old girl, I had convinced my father to take me to Graceland. I described our cross-country road trip from New Jersey to Memphis, including the car breaking down three times on our way to the king's mansion.

Cameron Craig, who read the post, felt an instant connection to the story and to me. He reached out over the phone to talk about how much the post meant to him, sharing that he felt the same way about Johnny Cash as I did Elvis. As we talked, we discovered we also had other professional experiences in common. This led to our collaborating to launch a conference called Binge Marketing. Set in Manhattan, the conference included mutual friends and speakers from both our networks—an impressive list of business leaders from IBM, eBay, DraftKings, and Apple, among others. Shared interests can often lead to successful business connections. In this case, I created a way to work together and a lasting business relationship.

Focus on Deeper Connections

It's not just who you know, it's how you know them. How many times has LinkedIn asked you to congratulate someone for something and you have no idea who they are? Instead of collecting LinkedIn contacts, focus on making deeper, more solid connections.

Dr. David Burkus, author of *Under New Management: How Leading Organizations Are Upending Business as Usual* and the organizer of the virtual Super Connector Summit, recommends what he calls the "shared activity principle": "Rather than invite someone to coffee, invite them into a project involving something they are passionate about, have some expertise in, and can contribute to," says Burkus. "You end up learning more about them and developing a deeper bond by partaking in an activity together than you do in just chatting."[2]

Get out of Your Comfort Zone

Burkus is not a big fan of joining networks in which everyone is on a similar wavelength. As he puts it, "These networks are echo chambers, and no new information or opportunities happen inside that echo chamber."

Networking is a topic Professor Ronald S. Burt, author, business consultant, and professor at the University of Chicago Booth School of Business, has been studying for years. As Burt observes, "People's relationships tend to cluster for different reasons: career, field of study, political ideology, gender, and so on."[3]

Gaps, or as Burt calls them, “structural holes,” exist between these clusters. Essentially, people within each cluster share the same perspectives and are blind to insights other clusters might offer. It is up to you to find the person or people who can help provide an introduction and bridge that structural hole. This is perhaps one of the most underutilized strategies for being persuasive. Bringing a variety of individuals and industries into your network helps you uncover new information, discover unexpected opportunities, and possibly even develop a whole new perspective.

For my agency, it was my mother. My mom is one of the most charismatic and convincing people I’ve ever met. I knew that all my clients would love meeting her because she is like a character out of a movie. I created an event and hosted it at our offices. My mom cooked her famous red sauce with spaghetti and meatballs. The event was called “Momma G, Meatballs, and Secrets to Success.” More than 100 people attended the event, and we held several more like it. There was a wait list every time. This was the perfect shared activity for me and my clients. They got to know me, my charming mom, and how I would help them be successful.

Search for the Uncommon Commonality

It’s only natural to be drawn to people whose experiences, memories, and emotions are similar to ours. When aiming to establish meaningful bonds with others, look for uncommon commonalities, those unique similarities people discover about themselves during conversation.

“Humans tend to cluster around common commonalities such as gender, industry, and ethnicity,” Burkus observes. “It’s the unexpected commonalities that are binding and give people more of a reason to stay in touch.”

Put People in Your Success Story

As a publicist, I've helped hundreds of obscure brands and executives become household names. My clients who have developed the most successful personal brands understand how to get people to back them consistently throughout their careers. They aren't quick to take credit for their own success, but rather show their network how they got there and why their supporters were integral to their meteoric rise.

The late motivational speaker Zig Ziglar once said, "You can have everything in life you want if you will just help enough other people get what they want."[4] We take this great advice one step further: not only do you have to help other people get what they want, you must make them believe that they have contributed to your success as well. What's more, you need to do so at the right points on your professional journey. If you wait too long, you'll be missing out on opportunities to be most convincing.

Business is all about give and take, but there is a shelf life for an ask. If you want reciprocity in business—you must act quickly. Research shows that if you do someone a favor in a professional setting, you only have a few hours to ask for a favor in return.[5] If you wait longer than that, the person's likelihood of doing you a favor back diminishes by almost half.

Sharing Your Ups and Downs

How you describe your professional wins or failures to others in your network creates a natural story arc. Sharing your ups and downs makes you instantly more convincing. You can talk about anything from launching a new business to debuting a product to seeking a challenge within your current job. Personal anecdotes build tension and interest and convey authenticity. If you are talking about a failure or setback, though, make sure to end the story with what you learned from the experience that's made you wiser and more effective.

Your strategy for getting people to back you and your professional wins depends on where you are in your career trajectory. Here's how to get others to get excited about your success at different points of your career:

- **It's just the beginning.** As you launch a new business or start your career, people typically root for you to succeed. They see you trying new things, and they are likely to show support. This is when people in your network are more likely to give you introductions, ideas, and ways to grow. The best convincers tell other people in their professional network about what they are doing, including their wins and struggles. This lets other people feel like they are in it with you.
- **Growing and learning.** Persuasive people know they can't take all the credit for their growth. They must show what they've learned and how it is changing them for the better. This is the stage in your career where you take classes, earn certificates, and showcase the expertise you are building. Examples of this include sharing small wins, new ideas, and social proof. Be candid about sharing a few self-deprecating anecdotes, jokes, and missteps—just don't overdo it to the point that you cast doubt on your own competence.
- **Taste of success.** This is the point in your career where you get to show off a bit. Cite case studies, insights, and industry support. Tout your achievements and demonstrate your confidence in what you know. At this

point, you are beginning to build your reputation as a thought leader in your niche or industry.

- **Reaching your potential.** At this stage in your career, the people who are happy for you feel your success is their success as well. Reinforce this by sharing specific ways other people helped you on your way up. Feel free to be candid about your hopes, dreams, and goals for the future, and don't be afraid to specifically ask others in your network for help in achieving your goals.
- **Send the elevator back down.** Mentor promising newcomers. Their success reflects well on you, as both a professional and a person. What's more, people you help professionally will often sing your praises and give you credit for the leg up. Oprah is masterful at this. She has an entire network of people who have been successful thanks to her promotion of their expertise. From Gayle King to Dr. Phil, she built a media empire while sharing the spotlight.

For most business professionals, growing a network is hard work. You hustle to meet as many thought leaders as possible in the shortest amount of time, make small talk, and rate your success according to the stack of business cards you've collected. But if you build your professional story, while telling others what is happening in a purposeful way, they will be more likely to help you when you need it.

Leverage the Majority Illusion

Social science calls the art of making something look more popular than it really is the Majority Illusion. This is one area where the questionable career advice "Fake it 'til you make it" has some actual relevance.

Whether you're trying to create a whole new category of contacts or connect to people in a particular company, make a point of asking your network who they know in that field or organization. This will earn you a handful of contacts that can serve as references or "brokers." Only ask people you know well, trust, and respect, because you should be ready to return the favor.

Uncovering the overlapping connections between yourself and people in your network can help you identify the major influencers in any industry. You'll benefit from the majority illusion as the influencers start to recognize your name on their contacts' feeds.

Don't Be Afraid to Add Tension

From the president of the United States to Marillyn Hewson, one of the highest-paid female CEOs, to billionaire sports team owner Ted Leonsis, all the prominent leaders I have worked with have mastered the art of building tension into the process of making high-stakes group decisions. They stress their teams to keep them performing at the highest level. Great leaders communicate their values, give their teams a decision-making matrix, and take a step back. When the pressure is on, or something goes against their values, they step in and provide guidance.

As the owner of a well-respected public relations firm, I was called in by Marillyn Hewson, the newly appointed CEO of Lockheed Martin, to help her prepare for and transition into her new role. She was looking for messaging and strategy to sell herself to the press as the right choice to lead the biggest defense contracting company in the world.

We met in a boardroom with an imposing dark mahogany table. Hewson was a tall, elegant woman. She wore a conservative St. John's suit, and her hair and makeup were flawless. When she walked into the room, it was clear she was in charge.

Everything about how she carried herself was purposeful. She sat directly across from me. There was tension in the room, but nothing I couldn't handle.

It soon became clear that she felt a little outside of her comfort zone when it came to being on camera in broadcast media. Her staff, led by a former Pulitzer Prize–winning print journalist, was extremely qualified to help her, but they struggled to please her. They needed reinforcements, which turned out to be me. There was no room for error—Hewson wanted to get her debut in the marketplace just right.

Hewson's internal communications staff had prepared an extensive media briefing book with over 30 pages worth of notes and guidance for working with reporters. She spoke not a word to me as she rifled through each page with a visible level of exacerbation and annoyance. She was overwhelmed and didn't feel ready. It was obvious to me that she thought she had to memorize a book worth of media material.

Without even introducing myself or my expertise, I said, "Let's begin by putting that book away. We are going to supply you with one page of no more than five sound bites for each interview you go on. Once you have those sound bites down, we will provide another page of the three to five most important facts and statistics the media will ask about. All the rest of the information is available if the reporter requests it after the interview is over. Sound good?"

Hewson's shoulders softened. She was relieved and she didn't miss the opportunity to tell her internal communications staff why.

"This is a teachable moment," she announced. "I never want to go into an interview feeling overwhelmed again. Make sure you take away how I want to be prepped in the future."

I felt a little anxious to have inspired such open and direct feedback. Her team didn't love it, but I smiled politely through the painful exchange. I couldn't help but notice that Hewson had made her point to her team with just the right amount of tension to get the results she wanted.

We then sat down together and wrote her talking points using words and phrases that matched her communication style. While we still covered the questions reporters would likely ask, she felt comfortable that the answers were in her executive voice.

Use Convincing Trigger Points

Back-to-back meetings, inboxes full of urgent emails, and the rise of remote work have made managing a team more challenging than ever before. A good leader must know how to identify and test convincing trigger points when trying to persuade their team to take on new projects, increase goals, or be more innovative.

This must be done using simulated experiences that are unrelated to the problem you are trying to get your team to solve. This approach is backed by Edward de Bono, who developed the theory of lateral thinking. The point of lateral thinking is that many problems require a different perspective to be solved successfully. That's why we put leaders in high-stress decision-making scenarios to test their thinking prowess. We create team-building events and workshops for leaders, online and in person. From role-playing with an actor playing a hostage taker in a bank robbery to getting a confession from an actor playing the role of a felon, these scenarios enable executives to understand how their team would react in new challenging and unfamiliar circumstances.

Leaders who go through the training come away feeling like they can take on any mundane day-to-day, difficult decision—because they have just learned how to successfully talk down a hostage taker or get a criminal to confess. The strategies they use in the training can be applied to any one of a hundred decisions they make every day in the business world. Knowing they can handle this level of stress with ease helps them feel ready to take on any business challenge that comes their way. Additionally, learning how to earn trust in a sensitive negotiation means communicating from a "we" instead of a "you" point of view.

TIPS FROM THE PODCAST WORLD'S MOST POWERFUL PERSUADERS

Successful interviews—like successful business interactions—start with establishing a trust connection. Podcast hosts like Lewis Howes and John Lee Dumas are naturals at getting people to drop their guard, relax, and tell stories listeners want to hear. So how do they do it, and what can we learn from their techniques?

With more than 5 million followers on social media and 300 million downloads for his podcast *The School of Greatness*, Lewis Howes is an internet sensation. Howes interviews experts and thought leaders from a variety of fields. No matter what field you're in, you can learn from one of his most effective tactics: asking his guests about their road to success.

According to Jason Feifer, editor in chief of *Entrepreneur* magazine, an approach like Howes's can be very useful in gaining trust and forging relationships. "Asking someone about their thought process regarding an idea shows you are taking an interest in them a deep and meaningful way, especially if you are able to extract an idea or concept from that method and have them explain it more."[6]

Using this tactic can help you raise dopamine levels in the brain of the person you are trying to convince. At once a hormone and a neurotransmitter, dopamine is part of the brain's reward system. Dopamine is known as the "feel good" hormone—levels go up when you experience pleasure, whether it's that first bite of chocolate cake, a new romance, or the knowledge that you are about to close a deal you've been chasing for months.

> **KEY POINT.** Acknowledge the challenges and praise the successes of the people you wish to convince. You will make them feel seen and respected. You may also get them to associate you with the dopamine jolt they get when you're around!

When John Lee Dumas launched *Entrepreneur on Fire*, podcasts were a relatively untapped content option. As Dumas puts it, "When I had the idea that I wanted to listen to a daily podcast, I went and searched for it. I found that it didn't exist. You need to find that void, that niche that's not currently being filled."[7] According to Dumas, filling a void is not enough. You need a passion for your subject matter.

Dumas believes you should be able to tell yourself, "This is something that I can really enjoy doing, not just today or tomorrow, but maybe even next year, three years from now." This authenticity spills over into why people will back you. That is how an unknown John Lee Dumas, working in a medium that was still in its infancy, was able to convince such diverse high-profile individuals as Barbara Corcoran and Tony Robbins to appear on his podcast.

KEY POINT. The more genuine authenticity and passion you display about your message, the more convincing you become.

Celebrities and industry tycoons often have a brand platform and messaging to support things that are important to them. *Shark Tank* investor Barbara Corcoran is no exception. Getting her to appear on his podcast was a major coup for Dumas. "I was watching an episode of *Shark Tank*," he recalls, "Barbara made the comment that she will do anything for our nation's veterans." As an eight-year combat veteran, Dumas knew he had his in. True to her word, Corcoran said yes to a vet, and Dumas got to record her live on the *Shark Tank* set! That interview became a huge credibility boost for both *Entrepreneur on Fire* and Dumas himself.

KEY POINT. Study what people value, especially if this is something they are very public about, like Corcoran's passion for helping vets. It's useful knowledge for your convincing tool kit.

Getting access to top-tier business celebrities like international self-help guru Tony Robbins is a challenge for anyone in journalism. In the early days of *Entrepreneur on Fire*, booking Robbins would have been a long shot. Instead, Dumas reached out to Robbins's son Jairek, who is following in his father's footsteps. During that interview, Dumas made a point of never mentioning Tony, focusing entirely on Jairek's career and achievements. A year after that interview, when Tony released his book *Money: Master the Game*, it was Jairek who suggested his father add *Entrepreneur on Fire* to the book tour. Getting on someone's radar may be a long game for convincing, but it just might pay off.

KEY POINT. Influence the people around those you want to convince.

RELATIONSHIPS, RITUALS, AND RESISTANCE

Unless your business is somehow 100 percent automated, there's a very good chance you rely on strong relationships to make things happen. In other words, the effectiveness of everything you do is often dictated by the strength of your relationships—be they with clients, potential collaborators, or colleagues. That's why making changes at the relationship level can have very powerful effects in your business.

Whether we notice it or not, our organizations (and our lives in general) are dictated by our daily rituals. The mindset is, "This is how we do things. This is how we've always done things. This is how we will always do things." This attitude leads to institutional inertia—which kills most ideas or initiatives before they even get off the ground. By examining company rituals and making strategic shifts to align them with our new objectives, we can coax ourselves and others into making required changes.

The key is to lower the perceived resistance behind the changes we propose. Resistance can stall even the best-laid plans. As it turns out, relationships can be one of the most effective ways to establish new rituals without introducing new resistance. The bigger the change, the more important this becomes. That's because when you implement a massive, sweeping change, you can expect massive, sweeping resistance. Ask yourself the following questions:

- How big is the change I'm recommending?
- What kind of resistance might it introduce as a result?

- What new values or priorities need to be in place to make this change happen?
- How can I take advantage of new roles or relationships to help everyone align around these values?

Do this and you'll be much farther ahead than leaders who fail to take these hidden (yet very real) psychological factors into account.

Relationship Conscience

A company we worked with used an interesting strategy to encourage new rituals, strengthen relationships, and reduce resistance to change in their corporate culture. It assigned an employee to be what the company called its "relationship conscience" for three months. During that whole quarter, that person's sole responsibility was to look at actions and decisions through a relationship-first lens. Every action was evaluated based on whether and how it improved relationships—with customers, with stakeholders, and with fellow employees.

Normally, these constant relationship reminders would have felt like nagging, but because everyone understood that this was an exercise with a positive end goal, the effect was the opposite. Team members were much more receptive to changes and recommendations coming from a person they interacted with daily rather than from a bulletin board or company email.

With everyone forced to rethink their actions through this relationship-first lens, what emerged was not just a new set of operations and procedures, but an entirely new culture—one that was aligned with the new direction the company was going in.

You may not be able to achieve a complete overhaul of your company culture, but you can change the way you approach relationships within your organization. Do this by drafting someone to help reinforce the new values you want to implement. For example, let's say your top priority is maintaining strong and authentic relationships with your customer base. Assign someone, preferably a well-liked and effective communicator, to the role of customer defender.

The customer defender's job will be to act as the personification of your most loyal and valued customer. Every action then needs to be filtered through the lens of, "Will this lead to an improved relationship with our loyal customers, or will it lead to frustration, resentment, or misunderstanding?"

Whatever your organization decides to implement during this time, you'll want to make sure you aren't ignoring the proven power of relationships to increase your odds of success.

KEY TAKEAWAYS

- There is a convincing sweet spot for both you and the person you are trying to convince where you express the right level of tension to communicate enthusiasm without being over-the-top. At the same time, you must raise the other party's tension level high enough to engage them just enough—but not so much that they start to feel threatened, manipulated, or stressed. We call this the Convincing Curve.
- While it's only natural to be drawn to people whose experiences, memories, and emotions are similar to ours, to create more lasting bonds, look for uncommon commonalities, those unique similarities people discover about themselves during conversation.
- Acknowledge the challenges and praise the successes of the people you wish to convince. You will make them feel seen and respected.
- When trying to forge a bond, study what people value, especially if it's something they are very public about.

CHAPTER 7

WHAT YOU CAN LEARN ABOUT CONVINCING FROM MAGICIANS, CON ARTISTS, AND FORTUNE TELLERS

"Did you hear the cops finally busted Madam Marie for telling fortunes better than they do?"

That famous line is from "4th of July, Asbury Park (Sandy)," Bruce Springsteen's classic ode to his favorite boardwalk on the Jersey Shore. I'm a Jersey girl myself. In fact, when I was in high school, our eccentric creative writing teacher invited her friend Madame Marie, the clairvoyant Bruce Springsteen immortalized in his classic ballad, to come talk to our class. For some reason, Madame Marie zeroed right in on young Adele Gambardella, aka yours truly. "I see a father figure whose name starts with a *J*," she intoned, staring straight into my eyes. "He's clutching his chest."

My mind was blown. My father's name is John, and he had just had a triple bypass. How could Madame Marie have known? Truth be told, she couldn't. But there are a lot of common male names—Jack, John, Jim, and so on. The father figure could have been a dad, a grandpa, a favorite uncle, even a mentor at work. And heart disease is certainly a common condition. Madame Marie was fishing, and I got hooked.

Fast-forward a decade. I was in my late twenties and on my evening commute from Manhattan back to New Jersey, when a well-dressed, well-spoken woman approached me. She said she was a frequent passenger on the 6:17 p.m. train. She had seen me before—she couldn't help but notice me in that stylish green wool coat I wore two days ago. She claimed she had lost her purse and needed train fare home to pick up her daughter. Exactly $17.25. Her seven-year-old daughter would be forced to wait out in the cold for over an hour if she didn't catch that train. I was immediately skeptical and yet . . . her story was so convincing. I pictured that poor frightened little girl, shivering in the cold. That woman had opened my heart and I opened my wallet.

When I got home that night, I told my roommate Queyn the story. "No way!" Queyn responded. "What did she look like?" When I described the woman, my friend confessed to having given that same woman the same exact train fare two days ago. How had we both been so easily conned? Let's examine some of the techniques she used:

- She raised any red flags about herself before I could, giving her enhanced credibility.
- She gave me a specific reason why she needed the money.
- She tapped into my capacity for guilt by evoking the picture of her daughter sitting out in the cold if I didn't provide her money.
- She had studied me in advance and described a coat I had worn a few days ago to make me think she was a commuter like me.
- She asked for exact fare, no more or less, so if I checked, her story would pan out.
- She appealed to my sense of being a good Samaritan.
- She forced a decision to provide her the money within 10 minutes of when the train was arriving.

HOW FORTUNE TELLERS, CON ARTISTS, AND MAGICIANS FOOL SMART PEOPLE

While the magician, con artist, and fortune teller have different objectives, they draw upon the same assortment of tricks to rope us in.

In the FBI, interrogations require special agents to read people accurately and fill in missing pieces of the puzzle. Whether it is trying to get someone to confess, flip a source, or simply convince a prosecutor it is time to make an arrest—cold reading is a critical skill for success.

Shotgunning is named for the way a shotgun fires a cluster of small projectiles in the hope that one or more of them will strike the target. The process involves the cold reader tentatively providing general information, some of which will be correct, or near correct, with the goal of provoking an emotional response. Madame Marie used this technique very effectively. A psychic can use shotgunning to work an entire audience. The odds are that someone in the room will have lost an older relative with a common name like "Mike" or "John." Other statements include things that are statistically more probable like:

- "I see a woman with blackness in the chest, lung cancer, heart disease, breast cancer."
- "I sense an older male figure in your life, who wants you to know while you may have had disagreements in your life, he still loves you."

Statements like these are intended to demonstrate that the fortune teller has mystical powers, but as we shall see later in this chapter, the technique can also be effective in personal situations like dating, dealing with your in-laws, or business situations that require forging a connection and maintaining trust.

THE BARNUM/FORER EFFECT

The Barnum effect, also known as the Forer effect, is a psychological phenomenon in which people attribute great accuracy to descriptions of their personality that are supposed to be tailored to them—think psychic reading, astrology, aura readings, and those irresistible personality tests on social media. In truth, these descriptions are nonspecific and general enough to apply to a broad range of individuals.

The $2 billion psychic industry, which includes fortune tellers, tarot card readers, mystics, and other "seers," is built on this technique. It doesn't hurt that, according to a recent poll cited by the Associated Press, roughly half of Americans believe in telepathy and precognition.

Good FBI agents tap into the Barnum/Forer effect when they conduct a suspect interview. The subject who is being interrogated wants the investigator to believe they weren't involved. They try to distance themselves from the crime in question. When Chip would ask probing questions about their involvement, the suspect would be purposefully vague. He'd claim to have been "in the bathroom" during the crime or incriminating conversation being discussed. When the suspect thinks you have a read on them and already know what they did, they are suddenly more forthcoming.

Chip would often start sentences with key phrases such as "at times," "you seem like," or "you pride yourself in" to give the conversation personal meaning. He often used the following statement to set up the conversation for maximum tension: "Listen, there are a lot of things I know and some things I don't. You are not going to know what those things are. So I am going to ask you questions, and this is how I am going to gauge your honesty." This type of statement unsettles suspects by creating the impression that the FBI knows a lot more than they do. In situations like these, what you don't say is just as or more important than what you do say, because the suspect is filling in the blanks.

According to "Your Brain on Magic," an article published in the *Atlantic Monthly*, February 13, 2015, "The study of magic . . . is the study of people and groups as much as it is of the senses and the firings of the brain; a magician looks at the whole as much as its parts."[1] In a 2007 interview for *Parade* magazine, famed illusionist Criss Angel revealed that, "A lot of the demonstrations that I do, when I get inside people's minds, is understanding human behavior and how people think and getting their patterns down. Many people say I'm really a student of humanity."[2]

At a magic show, the audience is in a fixed position for an illusion. For instance, the famed magician David Blaine asks people on the street to stand still while he pretends to levitate eight inches off the ground. He directs his audience and sets the rules so he can set up the trick. "This takes a lot of energy—bear with me—you've got to give me space," he insists. You fall for the illusion for the simple reason that you have been positioned. Since magic isn't real, it requires the magician to be able to use your own senses against you.

We all process our experiences according to a type of internal shorthand that allows for a quick interpretation of what our senses are telling us. Our belief that we can spot a trick, a con, or a lie is precisely what magicians, con artists, and fortune tellers use against us because they understand our default patterns of perception and thought.

Subjective validation is the human tendency to believe information that validates one's self-esteem. The Barnum/Forer effect is most powerful when communication involves a careful balance of validation and criticism, admiration and admonishment, confidence-boosting and codependency. People read their own personality into the communication, for better and for worse.

FORER STATEMENTS

Forer statements are basic personality descriptors, developed in a classic experiment by psychologist Bertram R. Forer, that resonate in a deep, personal way with all types of people.[3] These statements are quite general, yet people perceive them as revelatory, intimate truths about their deepest selves. While these statements are commonly used by psychics, tarot readers, fortune tellers, and yes, con artists, they remain useful tools for anyone who wants to understand—and convince—another person. Why? Because they make people feel seen and understood.

What can you learn from these statements, and how do they apply to business? Everything (see Table 7.1).

TABLE 7.1 Predictive Statements

Statement	Why It Works
You tend to be critical of yourself.	The underlying desired perception you are hitting is humility, but the downside of it could be insecurity.
You have a great deal of unused capacity, which you have not turned to your advantage.	People think they were destined for greatness or success, but they rarely do anything about it.
While you have some personality weaknesses, you are generally able to compensate for them.	Overcoming adversity, grit, and determination are built into this statement.
Although you are disciplined and self-control outside, you tend to be insecure and anxious inside.	This statement can reveal intellectual vanity, emotional weakness, and a feeling of exclusion or rejection.
At times you have serious doubts as to whether you have made the right decision or done the right thing.	You can use this statement to probe for decisiveness versus indecision. It's a good way to assess whether someone is risk averse.
You prefer a certain amount of change and variety and become dissatisfied when hemmed in by restrictions and limitations.	Is the person you are dealing with making excuses, laying blame, or avoiding responsibility? Do they chafe at rules or restrictions? This statement can help you find out.

(continued on next page)

Statement	Why It Works
You pride yourself as an independent thinker, and do not accept others' statements without satisfactory proof.	The upside of this statement can reveal certainty and intelligence. It's a good way to legitimize another's thinking. The downside could be that the person is stubborn and a control freak.
You have found it unwise to be too frank in revealing yourself to others.	This statement allows someone to see themselves as measured and mysterious. They can be very private, and this may raise an alarm.
At times you are extroverted, affable, and sociable, while at other times you are introverted, wary, and reserved.	The introvert will view this as validation that they manage to sometimes be open. The extrovert will be reassured that they don't always come on too strong or learn from their mistakes in oversharing. The downside is they may find it hard to see themselves as either-or.
Some of your aspirations tend to be unrealistic.	The implication here can be that the person has delusions of grandeur, but the statement may also reveal insecurity.
Security is one of your major goals in life.	People will see this as comforting because they may seem measured and predictable. The downside is that it may also seem like they aren't willing to strive for higher goals.

Take the statement, "You have a great need for people to admire you." Deep down, we all want to be validated and admired for something. My mother, Lorraine Gambardella, for example, loves being admired for her cooking. If you say something nice about my mother's cooking, she will go out of her way to remember specifically what dish you liked and have it ready for you every time you visit.

Using admiration also works in the office. I had an employee who took great pride in her editing skills. I sensed her desire for admiration and genuinely thought she was an exceptional editor. I once mentioned my admiration for her editing prowess in front of the entire office. After that, she went out of her way to edit everyone's work, ensuring no comma was never out of place. The entire office benefited.

In work and in life, we are frequently criticized for what we do wrong, instead of validated for what we are doing well. When you can be a source of positive affirmation for your clients, coworkers, or even your child, you will gain their goodwill and admiration. This alone could make you more persuasive than most people. This does not mean you should give people phony compliments. But if there is something a colleague, subordinate, or client does exceptionally well, praise them for it. You will reap the benefits.

Cold readers intuitively understand we all want to be noticed and validated for personality traits that others may not possess. When you veil a request in validation, it's much harder for people to turn you down. If the person feels like, "I am the best at this ________________" (fill in the blank)—it becomes part of their identity and inspires enthusiasm for the task.

Amazingly, Forer statements are equally effective whether you perceive what they reveal about you as a negative or a positive. When you use these statements toward others in your personal or professional life, you elicit a response. Whether that response is positive and open or negative and defensive, you learn something about the other person. And they will feel understood.

Forer statements reveal how people want to be perceived. Whether in our professional or private lives, we want to be admired, we want to release our untapped potential, and we want to feel like we make good decisions. We want to appear disciplined and to have self-control. We want to turn our weaknesses into strengths, and we need others to believe our weaknesses are correctable. Moreover, we want excuses for our shortcomings, whether we blame an individual or a given situation.

Why Forer Statements Are Effective

What can be more powerful than getting others to believe that the best version of themselves has yet to be revealed? Nothing.

Understanding people's motives is an essential critical skill, whether you are closing a sale, hiring a new employee, or wooing a potential mate. How do you figure out what motivates people? What's at the heart of their sense of self? And how can you channel those beliefs to be more convincing? The answer lies in how people want to be seen.

In a *Forbes* article entitled "This Is Your Brain on Storytelling: The Chemistry of Modern Communication," the author discusses the neurochemistry of storytelling.[4] When we first start paying attention, our brain releases cortisol, which helps us focus and stay alert. If we find a story intriguing and rewarding, the brain produces dopamine, which helps us maintain focus and stick with the story. "And then," the article states, "comes what could very well be the wonder drug of storytelling: oxytocin. While there are many other things in the human organism that help make us social, oxytocin has been identified as a chemical that promotes prosocial, empathic behavior." Oxytocin enables us to identify and sympathize with the "hero" of a story. When a person responds to a Forer statement, that hero is them, and they are primed for meaningful interaction with you.

HONING YOUR COLD READING SKILLS TO BECOME MORE CONVINCING

No matter your line of work, you're in the persuasion business. That requires the ability to read people with a certain level of accuracy. Unfortunately, most of us just aren't as good at reading others as we'd like to think.

Social psychologist William Ickes is known for his extensive research on "empathetic accuracy," also known as "everyday mind reading."[5] This is the ability to read another person's thoughts and emotions. Ickes's findings indicate that strangers read each other with an average accuracy rate of about 20 percent. Close friends and married couples are only slightly better at reading each other, with an accuracy rate of 35 percent. How can we increase our ability to read people more accurately? How can we enhance our cold reading skills to make us more convincing in business and in life?

Questions Are the Answer

In a business meeting or a negotiation, questions can help you determine intent and hidden meaning and discover how to get more of what you want. Just the fact that you are asking questions makes you appear interested, curious, and engaged (as long as you're not asking about something you should already know or have looked into).

Let's say you're a vendor trying to convince someone your company is the right choice. You must predict what the potential customer is feeling and commit to a reassuring level of certainty about their experience. You also need to gauge the amount of time they are willing to devote to hearing about your product or services. You can use the shotgun approach to elicit information about your prospect's previous experiences. Some guesses regarding your competition's shortcomings probably will resonate, or they wouldn't be considering a change. Use mathematical probabilities and industry standards to garner the best price, and don't hesitate to work in a Forer statement or two. You will recognize modified Forer statements in the last two sample questions that follow:

- "I've seen in the past with a company of your size that it spends between $30,000 and $60,000 on this type of service. Am I close?"
- "I sense that the last vendor you used didn't meet all your demands. While the project may not have worked completely—you did achieve some of what you wanted to—but that's why you are seeking other options. Is that correct?"
- "You pride yourself as an independent thinker and do not accept vendor promises without satisfactory proof . . . that's why we can provide you testimonials and case studies that demonstrate we are the right choice."
- "You have a great deal of unused capacity, which you have not turned to your advantage because you haven't had the right strategic partner."

Now let's explore how to apply this approach to a personal situation like getting to know someone you just started to date. You can begin with the usual getting-to-know-you questions—past relationships, how long they lasted, how they feel about dating, and so forth. You might ask about the longest relationship they were in and why it ended. Then based on what you've learned, you draw them out with some Forer statements, creating the impression that what you have just learned has given you a deeper insight into who they are. Try asking questions like these:

- "I am getting the sense you've have more long-term relationships than short ones. Is that right?" Use Forensic Listening to probe for more information before moving on to another question.
- "You seem like a confident person who knows what they want. I'm thinking you were likely the one who ended the relationship. Am I right?"

If your assumption is wrong, use strategic pauses to give them time to correct you and convey that you are thinking about what they have said.

Forer statements are also very effective in the context of a first or second date. Use them to show your date you're intuitively connected to their innermost feelings:

- "At times you are extraverted, affable, sociable, while at other times you are introverted, wary, and reserved."
- "You have found it unwise to be too frank in revealing yourself to others . . ."

The goal is to read the other person, win them over, and get them to potentially see you as someone they could have a relationship with in the future.

KEY TAKEAWAYS

- We all process our experiences according to a type of internal shorthand that allows for a quick interpretation of what our senses are telling us. Our belief that we can spot a trick, a con, or a lie is precisely what magicians, con artists, and fortune tellers use against us because they understand our default patterns of perception and thought.
- The Barnum Forer effect is a psychological phenomenon in which people attribute great accuracy to descriptions of their personality that are supposed to be tailored to them—which is why psychic reading, astrology, aura readings, and online personality tests are so popular.
- Forer statements are 12 basic personality descriptors developed by psychologist Bertram R. Forer that resonate in a deep, personal way with all types of people and elicit revealing information. While these statements are commonly used by psychics, tarot readers, fortune tellers, and con artists, they are useful tools for anyone who wants to understand—and convince—another person.
- To convince others, we must be able to read them with a certain level of accuracy. Most of us just aren't as good at reading others as we'd like to think. Forer-type statements stimulate revealing responses that can help us understand others more fully.

CHAPTER 8

THE NEUROSCIENCE OF CONVINCING

It was an early morning apprehension, but the FBI and local police were there in force, with helicopters and several squad cars. A portion of the city was on lockdown while our suspect was on the loose. Our team was there to make an arrest and the bad guy wasn't home. The FBI team knocked on a bunch of the doors in the fugitive's neighborhood and obtained a cell phone number for the suspect. Chip was armed with a hostage negotiator's best weapon, a cell phone. Chip's job: to get this guy to turn himself in.

Chip called the number and heard the other line pick up, but there was just silence. He did not know who answered but decided to take his chances.

"Hi Jeff," he began. "My name is Chip, I am from the FBI, and I am here to help you today." He waited a while. There was no response, so that forced him to talk.

For those who have broken the law, the initials FBI evoke a host of emotions—various combinations of anxiety, mistrust, hostility, and fear. Chip decided to try and go for an immediate emotional connection with the fugitive.

"Jeff, how bad does your life suck right now?" Chip asked. After a long 15 seconds, the guy answered. "What's your name again?"

Once the suspect talks, they have decided to engage with the negotiator. This significant change in the conversational dynamics was an indication that Chip had made progress and broken through the subject's stress to establish a neurological connection.

"Jeff, no doubt you are aware that we are at your apartment." Chip said. Nothing from the other end. "I am standing near your apartment, and I see a pizza place down the street. I wonder if you have ever gotten a slice there, Jeff. What kind of slice would you get?" No response.

While this may seem like a crazy question to ask a violent fugitive in the middle of a standoff, it is a strategic approach rooted in neurological principles. Hostage negotiators are trained to listen more than they talk. When they do choose to speak, they usually try to get the hostage taker to share a story. The goal is to establish a path of possible trust within 10 to 12 seconds.

That's why Chip chose to ask about a restaurant located a few yards from his house. If you have ever lived in the New York City metro area, you'd know that the type of slice someone gets says a lot about them. New Yorkers feel a personal attachment to the type of pizza they like. The sauce-to-cheese ratio and topping preference become a signature personality trait. Chip hoped this question would attach to a memory and create an emotional connection with the fugitive. When the pizza connection attempt didn't illicit a response, he knew he needed a different way to connect.

Looking around, he noticed a pair of sneakers dangling from the telephone wires outside the suspect's window. "Just noticed those Nikes hanging from the telephone wire above your house. Are those your shoes up there?" Chip asked. Still no response.

These two initial questions were an attempt to build a relationship quickly, but not too quickly. Next, Chip's goal was to show him that he understood what the suspect must be going through.

"We know everything about your case," Chip declared. "I know what it must be like to be on the run. Your stress is off the charts. You can't get a regular job. You're relying on friends who just might decide to turn you in for the reward money. You can't even call your mom because we might have her phone tapped. You have to pay cash for everything. I bet your funds are running out. You don't even know where to lay your head at night. On top of all that, you're worried about what could happen if you get stopped by the cops. Once they run your name or information, things can turn bad for you really fast. Does that sound about right?"

The suspect had been a fugitive from the FBI for more than eight months, and the charges he was facing were not going away. It's emotionally debilitating to be on the run for that long. To get him to give himself up, Chip had to build a "Trust Narrative" to establish an emotional connection.

THE TRUST NARRATIVE

Hostage negotiators are trained to use the pitch, tone, and cadence of their voice to convey empathy and concern and de-escalate a volatile situation. Using a lower, slower tone when dealing with violent people helps create a sense of calm. Successfully implemented, this can result in the person seeing you as someone they could trust over time. The negotiator then uses a Trust Narrative to quickly assess the underlying desires of the person under duress.

"To establish a rapport with my fugitive," Chip recalled, "I demonstrated that I understood the dangers and challenges of life on the lam. I could describe the guy's pain better than he could. This is pivotal in building a connection. At work or at home, whenever someone you are trying to connect to is in a heightened emotional state, try to connect them to a story that represents their perception of reality."

Using the Trust Narrative in Business

In business, you can use the trust narrative to get to what's important for the person you are trying to convince. There will be multiple doors, each with a different possible outcome, and each outcome will produce a different emotion such as fear, indifference, excitement, joy, and so on. The best convincers know which doors to open first and how to build a path forward. In the case of the fugitive, the emotion was desperation. He was trapped, and he knew it. By describing his predicament in an empathetic way, Chip established trust and demonstrated the futility of continuing to resist. It gave him the out he desperately needed.

FOUR STEPS TO GET OTHERS TO COME TO YOU

For the purposes of practical business applications, we've broken down the steps Chip used to interview high-value subjects back in his FBI days. The principles of connection are the same in any business situation. If the FBI interviewer wants to get to the truth, obtain a confession, or garner details of a crime, they must create an atmosphere in which people feel they can be open and forthcoming.

Step 1: The Dial-in Method

By dialing in to someone's situation, you make them feel like they matter. Your focused attention demonstrates that you've taken the time to understand and empathize with what they might be experiencing during your interaction. This helps someone feel heard and truly seen. One of the most powerful ways to show you are dialed in is to selectively repeat what the other person is saying. For example, if someone you are meeting with shows up late and tells you they were stuck on the bridge for an hour, you might empathetically exclaim, "A whole hour? How awful." But beware, or as actor Matthew McConaughey likes to say, "Don't half-ass it."

We've taught the Dial-in Method as part of the Convincing Company's executive training, and I will never forget the tech-entrepreneur who came up to me and said, "I tried it, and it doesn't work!" "It does work," I replied. "Why don't you tell me in detail how you implemented it, and I can tell you where you might have gone wrong?"

The guy told me his fiancé came home one night venting about her terrible day at work. He decided this might be a good opportunity to try the techniques he had learned in our training. The conversation went like this:

The fiancé: "I had the worst day ever."

The entrepreneur: "The worst day ever."

The fiancé: "Yes, my boss came out of his office and started yelling at me for no reason."

The entrepreneur: "For no reason."

The fiancé: "Yeah, and he humiliated me in front of all my coworkers."

The entrepreneur: "All your coworkers."

The fiancé: "You aren't really listening to me. You're just repeating the last few words I am saying like a parrot."

Trying not to laugh, I asked him for a little more clarification. What was he doing while his fiancé ranted about her awful day? It turned out he'd been lying on the bed texting the whole time.

The entrepreneur made two mistakes. First, he was too literal in taking our advice. Repetition works when used sparingly. The person feels heard. He overdid it, which is why he sounded "like a parrot." He could just as easily have replaced some of the repetition with short phrases like "That's awful." Or "I hate when that happens." Just as important was the fact that he was texting. He was distracted, and his fiancé knew it. It's hard to feel heard by someone who won't look up from their phone.

When someone senses that you aren't really dialed in to the conversation, it makes them feel like you don't value what they have to say. You must be present and focused without distractions.

Step 2: Collaborate with Them

To demonstrate how to use this step, Chip takes us back to a time when he was the special agent in charge of garnering two confessions.

"In the criminal and legal world, a proffer session is a meeting between the subject of a federal criminal investigation, the person's attorney, and the prosecutor or special agent on the case," Chip explained. The case in question was a factoring case. Factoring is when someone uses a private company to give them funds ahead of monies owed to them from clients or other business dealings. Plainly stated, businesses can get money in advance of receiving a payment by using a factoring company. As you can imagine, this is often an opportunity for fraud.

"On the case I was assigned," Chip recalled, "two District of Columbia government employees were accused of fraud. Pretending to be business associates, they had applied for money and provided false documentation for their claims."

To process these claims, the factoring company required identification and proof that the claims were legitimate. Since the two fraudsters were employees of the District of Columbia, they had access to blank letterhead memos for the transaction and were able to forge memos of understanding, a letter of intent, and an invoice for services allegedly rendered.

The government employees provided their fake documents to the factoring company. They had already received four payments totaling $325,000 before the factoring company started to suspect something wasn't right.

After doing a little investigating on his own, the president of the factoring company reached out to the FBI. It didn't take long to identify the two DC government employees responsible for the fraud. The U.S. Attorney's Office decided to charge each defendant separately. Each defendant had an attorney, and the attorneys agreed to separate proffer sessions for each of their clients. Chip remembers:

There were five people in each session: the defendant, their attorney, the DC inspector general, me, and another investigator. The first defendant was a woman we will call Valerie. She vehemently insisted that she was completely unaware of the fraud happening around her. We showed her paperwork that had her signature on it. She responded that she trusted the other defendant, who had told her that the paperwork was in order. She said he pressured her because their boss, a public official, wanted the payment to be processed without the proper paperwork. She agreed to approve the paperwork. She said that was the last she heard of anything until investigators started asking questions.

As we questioned Valerie, she played the part of an innocent person, falsely accused, yelling, and pounding the table in anger. She thought her fervor would persuade us that she wasn't guilty. The more facts we presented, the more hostile she became. She cried, screamed, and protested her innocence regardless of what we asked her—every reaction was a 10 out of 10.

Valerie denied any involvement in the scam, but the facts suggested otherwise. We had discovered a large sum of money in her bank account. When I asked her where it came from, she claimed she had inherited the money. I asked the logical question: Who died? She responded by screaming, but she couldn't provide a name. A few things were at play during this interrogation:

- Valerie was trying to fool me with her histrionics.
- Her body positioning was at odds with her words.

- She was consistently nonspecific about details—such as who supposedly left her with the large sum sitting in her bank account.
- When she retold her story, parts the original version dropped out in the retelling.
- She harbored a grudge against her co-conspirator.

When we interviewed Defendant #2, whom we will call John, his position was that he had no idea how any of this had happened. Yes, he'd seen the paperwork, but he had no idea who the actual criminals were. Certainly not him—he was only doing his job. What John didn't know was that Valerie was blaming him. They were being tried and questioned separately, but we had information from both their bank accounts. There was no plausible explanation as to why either of them would have that much money.

John was still denying any involvement in the crime when Chip told him he had been fingered by Valerie. It started to dawn on him that his story was falling apart, and finally, he showed signs that he was about to break. This included looking down more, shaking his head, and disconnecting from the conversation. It was clear he wanted to be anywhere but there.

Even the guiltiest people crave empathy. They want to be listened to and understood. John was no exception. "I'm in here and I am nervous," John admitted. "I am an innocent person, and I don't do things like this."

"John knew he was in trouble," Chip recalled. "We were telling him what our investigation found. We would show him the documents and ask him why his signature was on it. Then we asked him about the large sum of money in his bank account. Unfortunately for him, he knew he had no good answers to defend his actions."

Step 3: Affirm That You Understand the Chain of Events

This interview was going nowhere, so Chip decided to shake things up. He got up and joined John on his side of the table.

"Listen, John," he said, "It's clear to all of us here that you are not a bad guy. You got caught up in something, and you don't know what to do or say. I am guessing you needed the money. You don't strike me as someone who wants to go out and buy a fancy car."

John was looking down, shaking his head, and trembling. He knew he'd been found out. Chip kept talking. "We don't want you to be charged for something you didn't do on your own. We have an idea of what went down, but we need you to tell us everything that happened. Valerie is saying you put her up to this. Eventually, she's going to say the whole thing was your idea."

That's when John laid everything out. "You are right," he said. Turning to his attorney, he asked, "Is it OK if I reveal everything that happened?" The attorney agreed, and we got the confession.

In Chip's handling of John, he acknowledged John's self-image as basically a decent person. John had committed a crime, but he was not a hardened criminal. By saying that he suspected John needed the money, Chip enabled John to feel a little better about himself. This gave him permission to open up and tell us the truth.

Empathy is a powerful tool for connecting, in business and in life. When you indicate that you know what someone is experiencing or share a story about a friend who's been in similar circumstances, you create an emotional connection. This will make you instantly more persuasive with anyone, in almost any business situation.

Step 4: Use Group Activities

Dr. Platt, the neuroscientist we interviewed about his theory of synchrony, suggested group activity as one way of encouraging syncing in a work environment. The group activity, such as a cooperative game or day of service, should have a shared goal and be followed by a debrief, which gives feedback on the outcome. The debrief emphasizes the strengths and weaknesses of the group effort.

Storytelling is another area that pulls us into the synchronized brain state. Similar to the debrief described earlier in this chapter, storytelling allows for a group to focus on the speaker. Eye contact and emotional connection help stitch the individuals in the audience together and synchronize their brains.

One obvious positive is that the group will have a temporary boost in morale. But the more important benefit is that by syncing as a team, the group is being prepared for their next win.

CONNECTING WITH SOMEONE WHO IS BEING DECEPTIVE

When a person is avoiding the truth or they are a bad actor and are hiding their actions, the interviewer needs to ratchet up the tension. Let's say the person in front of you is loud, aggressive, insulting, or demeaning. Contrary to popular advice, you do not want to match their intensity or mimic their behavior.

Instead, increase tension by remaining measured in your voice's pitch, tone, and cadence. Talk slowly or quicken your pace to create dissonance. Keep to the facts, stay logical, and point out what the other person is not addressing and most likely avoiding.

HOW STORIES ACTIVATE THE BRAIN

According to Richard Branson, "Entrepreneurs who cannot tell a story will never be successful." Throughout this book, we use stories from our respective careers to illustrate our convincing techniques. Stories are a way of bringing ideas to life and keeping others engaged. That engagement is based in our biology. Recent research in psychology and neuroscience conducted at Princeton University revealed that a listener's brain waves actually start to synchronize with those of a storyteller as a story progresses.

According to a study by Greg J. Stephens, Lauren J. Silbert, and Uri Hasson, "neural coupling"[1] or "mirroring" occurs across many different areas of the brain and can induce a feeling of a shared experience. When we are hearing a story, the motor and sensory cortices, as well as the frontal cortex are all engaged. The study explains that "these neural networks are nurtured by feelings of anticipation of the story's resolution, involving the input of your brain's form of candy, dopamine."

Research indicates that when we hear an emotionally charged story, our brains release excess dopamine, making it easier to remember something with greater accuracy. This may hark back to our hunter-gatherer days, when outsmarting a large animal meant life, death, or dinner for the whole tribe.

CONVINCING, TIMING, AND NEUROSCIENCE

As much as we'd like to think our charm, good looks, and approachability make us naturally persuasive, research shows it's not that simple. The other person's ability to neurologically receive the message is a critical part of persuasion that can't be overlooked.

Recent neuroscience research supports this idea. "Too much glutamate in your system affects your lateral prefrontal cortex—the part of the brain responsible for decision-making and planning—in a significant way," according to a study published in 2022 in *Current Biology*.[2] If your glutamate levels are too high or you work too hard on very difficult tasks (more than 6.5 hours), there's a buildup that impairs your decision-making ability. The fatigue made study participants opt for easier, less demanding work physically and mentally. As they grew more tired, participants in the study made decisions faster and were more likely to take shortcuts.

This is where timing factors into convincing. Your timing needs to change depending on what type of idea, product, or service you are pitching and your prospect's level of fatigue and stress.

For instance, if it is a complex sale that requires different decision makers, consider reaching out in the morning or right after lunch. If you are making a presentation or pitching a client, morning meetings are recommended to get the freshest version of your investor or prospect. This is when they are more likely to be refreshed, ready, and willing to think about a decision. Approach them with just the right amount of pushback, strategically timed for them to be neurologically ready to think—as opposed to later in the day when they may be fatigued.

However, if you are selling a service that offers shorter-term benefits or payoffs, such as training, it might be worth delaying that sales call, advertisement, or email until the later in the afternoon. Neuroscience studies show people are more likely to make impulse purchases when they are tired or experiencing decision fatigue. The same would hold true for a leader who wants to get his board of directors to make a rapid decision. Ideally, the leader would present the board with several small decisions first, leaving the decision they want to get approved fast for last.

In the next chapter, we will explore how to read people effectively and how to master the art of opening the right door at the right time.

KEY TAKEAWAYS

- When someone is in a heightened emotional state, try to establish an empathetic connection to their concerns, feelings, and perception of reality.
- The Dial-in Method entails a complete focus on a person's situation, giving them your full attention, and validating and affirming their thoughts and feelings.
- It's important to consider timing and the type of idea, product, or service you're pitching when trying to convince someone. For example, if it is a complex sale with a variety of decision makers, consider reaching out in the morning or right after lunch.
- For a less complex pitch where a quick decision is likely, consider delaying the call until later in the afternoon. Neuroscience studies show people are

more likely to make impulse purchases when they are tired or are experiencing decision fatigue.

- Good stories facilitate convincing because the listener's brain waves actually start to synchronize with those of a storyteller as a story progresses.

CHAPTER 9

THE BUSINESS BENEFITS OF FBI BEHAVIORAL ANALYSIS

This chapter aims to give you the same set of tools the FBI uses to analyze behavior, and you don't have to be a special agent to learn how to use them! This is something you already know how to do, maybe just not on a conscious level. When your best client launches a Zoom meeting, do you immediately know their state of mind? What about your boss? Can you discern their mood the minute they walk in the door in the morning? Is the look on your assistant's face enough to tell you he's about to break some bad news?

Chip and I have asked many of our clients these types of questions, and the answer is always yes. Not mostly, usually, or sometimes—always. I bet you're nodding your head in agreement right now. What accounts for this? How is it that everyone we ask responds the same way? The truth is you can read people. You just don't understand how you're doing it or how to cultivate this power and call on it when needed.

Think about the people whose behavior you can predict. Your boss. Your significant other. Your kids. Your best friend. Your business partner. What all these people have in common is the fact that you've known them over time. You've learned their patterns of behavior, and the longer you know them, the more predictable they become.

In business, you don't necessarily have the advantage of knowing someone well enough to sense their moods or predict their reactions. In this chapter, we are going to teach you how to observe people in various contexts (e.g., at work, in social situations, under stress, with superiors or underlings). You will learn a couple of FBI techniques to read people's psychographic details such as personality, lifestyle, attitudes, aspirations, values, and interests.

The Pattern of Life is a deep dive, best saved for someone who is going to have an ongoing impact on your business or career. The Mind Map is a more top-level approach that can be very useful when preparing for a first encounter.

IDENTIFYING SOMEONE'S PATTERN OF LIFE

When the FBI is putting together a profile of a suspect, the goal is to get a sense of their Pattern of Life (POL). Before any subject interview, Chip would do as much research on the target as he had time for. Not all subject interviews require this type of research up front, but a violent drug kingpin or a million-dollar fraudster? Absolutely.

Chip's due diligence would always start with the obvious—basic information gleaned from social media, various records checks, or interviews of people who may know the subject to put together the target's psychographic information. But all that is just low-hanging fruit. POLs strive to look at the individual from a day-to-day perspective. The goal is to use those observations to build the subject's psychographic profile. The same principles apply to what you are trying to do when you are reading people in a business context. What changes is how you develop the data.

Our intention was to build the strongest possible base for an interview, Chip recounted. "Some of the info you glean is practical. Let's say I'm going to schedule a morning interview. I will need to know what time my subject leaves the house in the morning. Do they stop for coffee along the way? If I saw evidence that my target wasn't a morning person, I could use that. Depending on my strategic goal, I might stick to scheduling our conversation bright and early. Or I could talk to them after lunch when they are fully awake and more relaxed."

Of course, the POL goes much deeper than finding out whether the subject is a lark or a night owl. As Chip describes it, we're looking for the person's attitudes, aspirations, values, beliefs, who they are in private. How do they respond to stress, embarrassment, or poor treatment? How do they wield authority? How do they relate to those who have authority over them? How do they want to be perceived by others?

The POL delves into multiple aspects of the suspect's life:

- **Stress level.** How do they drive? Are they a smoker? Do they drink too much? Do they appear highly emotional?

- **Adherence to conventional norms.** Do they spend time with their family or hang out with their fellow criminals? Do they go to religious services? Are they a team player? Are they punctual? Polite? Do they tip well?
- **Degree of loyalty or disloyalty.** Does it appear from other intel that they are looking to move up in the organization? Are they cheating on their wives or girlfriends? Are they plotting to make a move on leadership? Do they skim money from the enterprise? Do they hold resentment against anyone within? Who and why? Have they talked about getting out?
- **How they unwind.** What are their rituals after leaving work? Do they have hobbies? Do they go to the gym or stop at the bar?
- **Communication style.** Do they prefer to talk, text, or interact in-person? How do they treat others they deem to be of lower position? Are they big talkers or quiet and guarded?

We are not suggesting that you follow people around like an FBI agent. However, these types of questions often answer themselves as you flesh out a person's psychographic profile over time. You're building a profile to understand someone in a granular way, so take notes after every encounter. Chip says you never know what might be important in the context of the target or the case. The same applies to your business.

THE POL, BUSINESS EDITION

Now let's look at how identifying a POL and creating a psychographic profile could work using your boss as a subject. You can start with the information that is readily available to you.

Communication Style

Observe the way your subject interacts with the team. This includes in-person meetings, conference calls, one-to-one interactions, conversations with vendors, and those dreaded Zoom calls. What format seems to make them most comfortable? What context is most likely to result in real action—a status meeting involving the whole team, a smaller project meeting, or a one-on-one with the door shut? Note their demeanor and disposition when they are about to deliver bad versus good news. Are there warning signs you can look out for? Is bad news delivered in a meeting or via email?

Emails

Emails are a fantastic source of data to which you have unlimited access. Your boss's emails may contain his or her thinking about the business, competition, customers/clients, market, appropriate and inappropriate behavior, future ambitions/targets/goals, new office developments, change in direction/emphasis, long-term plans, personnel changes, strategic thinking . . . the list goes on. Because business emails are a controlled form of self-expression, they won't give you much insight into someone's inner thoughts and feelings. What they do reveal is how someone wants to be perceived. Here are a few more "tells" you can glean from emails and texts:

- Who has been excluded from the chain?
- If you get cc'd a lot, notice whether the content and style of the emails change depending on who's been looped in.
- Keep an eye out for sarcastic or passive-aggressive wording.
- Do they use emails to praise and encourage people?

- What type of content to they focus on—what gets them commenting and emailing?

Not all this information will be useful, but the process and rigor of forcing your mind to think through these communications will bear fruit in the future.

Outside the Office

There is also a huge amount of information you can pull from out-of-office activities, whether it's an intimate client lunch, after-work happy hour, a conference out of town, or a company bonding retreat. Put on your metaphorical FBI jacket and pay attention to the details. Watch how the person you are observing treats the waitstaff. Do they send food back? Are they demeaning? Does their behavior toward you change? Do they try to put you in a positive light before a client or your colleagues and make an effort to bring you into the conversation?

Examine What They Emphasize

Tracking your boss's office behavior over time will provide insight into what he or she values. A generous, nurturing type will elevate people in the retelling of events. They will reward the team for working all weekend or pulling an all-nighter, as opposed to acting like that's just part of the job. They may act as a mentor to a young employee.

Keep an eye out for problematic behavior. For example, if the boss is mentoring someone, is the mentee truly deserving? Are they a sycophant who spends their work time listening to the boss's war stories? When the most useless people in the office start hanging out in the corner office all the time, that's an indication that the boss has a fragile ego.

Does your boss refer to specific books or individuals as professional examples and inspiration? Familiarize yourself with these books or individuals, and see whether their influence translates to the atmosphere at work. Maybe your boss just wants to signal that they are following the latest influencer without actually implementing their advice. Compiling these observations will help you understand the big picture and predict future behavior. How and why things happen, who gets promoted, and who gets overlooked—it will all become clear. And you will know whether to keep angling for that promotion or put your résumé together.

A Problematic Boss

Amelia, a client of ours, was having difficulty with her direct supervisor, Janice. Janice seemed erratic, unpredictable, and often hard to handle. Her feedback was not constructive. To understand the issue, we recommended that Amelia observe Janice's behavior during the day. We were building Janice's POL and nothing was off the table. We asked a lot of questions.

Problematic Boss Checklist

- Did Janice interact with people in the morning, or was she glued to her phone? What was her expression? Did she have anything to eat, or was coffee her breakfast?
- How many meetings did she have each morning? Did she prefer to meet in her office or in someone else's? Was her door open or closed?
- When did she break for lunch in the afternoon? How long did it take? Or did she choose to eat at her desk alone?

- How did she interact with others in meetings? Did she seem to have favorites?
- How did her supervisors treat her? Was she underappreciated or highly respected?
- Did she check in on Amelia and her work?
- What time did she come in? Was she punctual? Did it annoy her when others were not? Was she chronically late? What time did she leave?
- When she would get upset, was it something someone said or did internally?
- What was going on in Janice's personal life that might impact her behavior?

First, we wanted to see if there were there some misperceptions about Amelia's performance that needed to be addressed. We asked her to describe when Janice was most upset with her. That's when it dawned on Amelia that Janice was especially volatile when she missed a specific payroll deadline. We suggested that Amelia assist her boss by regularly reminding her of the deadline. This helped a bit, but Janice was clearly still not a fan of Amelia.

What Amelia didn't realize was that making her boss feel supported and appreciated was part of her job. Until she started doing this effectively, Janice would continue to have doubts about Amelia. Additionally, Amelia noticed that for the past four weeks, Janice had frequently been coming in early and leaving late. Each time she would return to the office, it took Janice a ton of time to catch up on emails and reprioritize her day. Whenever this happened, Janice was flustered and angry and did not give Amelia constructive feedback.

Amelia began implementing our recommended approach. She realized that her boss was more of an evening person and didn't really like doing hard tasks until after 3 p.m. By the way Janice kept her desk and often misspelled words in emails, we deduced she was a bit disorganized and lacked attention to detail when in a rush. Amelia also noticed that Janice got upset easily when she missed meetings or deadlines. She didn't have the time or inclination to tell Amelia how she could help her. However, the meetings and deadlines she missed pertained to Amelia's responsibilities.

There was one guy Janice liked. His name was Chris, and Janice would praise him in emails and in-person meetings. While Amelia was slightly nauseated by Chris, she went through the emails and noticed a pattern. Chris would take on what he knew Janice wanted him to complete and anticipate the next step without being asked. He just "seemed to know" how to handle the boss.

Amelia asked Chris what might be impacting Janice. He said, "Oh, she has two sick parents, and she is the primary care provider. When she comes back from the visits at the assisted-living facility, she is drained and overwhelmed. It takes her a long time to get caught up with what's happening in the office. She really appreciates when I can summarize and report on what's happening when she is away, because it makes her life much easier. She didn't ask me to do it, but I know it makes a big difference."

How Amelia Adjusted Her Approach

After reviewing Janice's POL, Amelia began to give Janice reports before they were due so that she would be better prepared for her meetings, especially on days she came in early or late. Amelia realized that Janice was disorganized, due to the stress of the visits with her ailing parents, so she gave her several reminders about deadlines with mitigation. She started praising

Janice to others at the office over emails. She gave her options when asking for her input, just like Chris did. All of a sudden, Janice started treating Amelia much better.

Amelia was finally doing things the way Janice wanted them done. When work relationships fall out of sync, it's often because one party feels misunderstood. Amelia had just been fulfilling her job description with no regard to how her work impacted her supervisor. Once that changed, the relationship flourished.

WATCH THE FAVORITES

We've talked quite a bit about observing the person you want to influence and convince—it could be a client or your boss. You can also glean a lot from observing interactions between them and someone they like and trust, such as a protégé or confidant. Watch how the favorites handle themselves during those interactions. You can learn from that person's behavior.

Watch the Favorites Checklist

- Do they stand in the boss's office differently?
- Do they use humor to facilitate the conversation?
- What is the pitch, tone, and cadence of their voice?
- Are they a sycophant, or do they voice counter ideas or opinions?
- Do they use mirroring in both word choice and what they wear? (Mirroring is when you look and sound like the people you are interacting with.)
- Do they interact with the boss with deference, or take a more egalitarian approach?

- Are they more likely to listen and ask thoughtful follow-up questions or seek to be heard?
- Does their demeanor change when they aren't in front of the boss?

Following the lead of someone who already knows how to handle your client or supervisor can be a shortcut to more successful interactions. With careful observation, in just a few days you can achieve a connection that could have taken weeks or months to build.

MIND MAPPING

Putting together a POL takes time and opportunity, but what if you need to get a quick take on someone you've never met? This is where we can learn from another technique called Mind Mapping. Think of it as your own private suspect board. Here, Chip takes us through the Mind Mapping process for one Jasper Hampton, a 31-year-old white male living in New York:

> I'm investigating him as a player in a cocaine operation that sells to high-income people in the financial sector. First, I write his name, right in the middle of a sheet of paper. Then I draw a short line from any point of the circled name and write something I know about him. He's single. He appears to be straight. He lives alone in a swanky apartment complex on the Upper West Side. He drives a brand-new Porsche 911. I know from his social media that he's a fancy dresser who frequents the hottest clubs and sits in the VIP area. I add all this to my map.

Now, I have a baseline to start making some Informed Assumptions. He may be actively dating and could have an account on Tinder or another dating ap. Since he's single in the city and not strapped for cash, he likely eats out a lot. Where does he do his clothes shopping—what kind of money is he spending? He's fit and muscular and posted a couple of selfies flexing at the gym—perhaps he meets some of his clients there. He labels a post of himself with some other guys, the "Ex-brokers club." Did he once have a broker's license? Does he have a connection to a large Wall Street firm? The other guys in the picture could be worth investigating, too.

What did I learn from this quick Mind Mapping exercise? Since clubbing is so prominent in Jasper's life, he likely conducts drug transactions at the clubs. I would consider inserting an undercover agent to do some controlled buys from him and his associates. It's hard to consistently sell drugs at a club without the manager knowing about it, so I would investigate a possible business relationship between Jasper and the club owner, manager, or maybe both. This might call for having an undercover agent get a job in Jasper's favorite club. Perhaps we can get a window into the size of Jasper's organization and find out who is in charge, who is mid-level, and who is lower-level or associate. Maybe we come across someone who is dissatisfied with the current leadership and might want to run his mouth about it.

All this gave Chip insight into what Jasper's psychographic profile might look like.

In a business setting, psychographics is often used to understand consumers based on their activities, interests, and opinions. "It goes beyond classifying people based on general demographic data, such as age, gender, or race," according to the research firm CB Insights.

> Psychographics seeks to understand the cognitive factors that drive consumer behaviors. This includes emotional responses and motivations; moral, ethical, and political values; and inherent attitudes, biases, and prejudices. Just because two people are roughly the same age and earn similar annual incomes doesn't mean they share similar political views or personal values, for example.[1]

Chip continued his analysis of Jasper:

> Young adult males typically follow stories and possessions representing power. The high-end cars, weight lifting, and drug crew all are in keeping with that. Likely guns are a part of this culture, as well. What about his values? Keeping the "code," looking out for his crew, being respected, and seen as "hard." Would he have ambitions beyond his level or rank in this organization? All this would be extremely useful to know in preparation for his interview and maybe getting him to flip.

Mind Mapping Your Potential New Client

Let's say you are a software as a service (SAS) supplier to HR departments for companies with over a thousand employees. You have been assigned a new territory in the southeastern seaboard. Your sales manager has given you a list of customers who didn't renew contracts within the last two years. She wants you to reach out to each one and get a meeting with a decision maker to find out why they didn't renew and what can be done to bring them back. Your team is tasked with returning with $750,000 worth of signed contracts for these nonrenews—in 30 days.

The first thing to do is schedule a meeting with your salespeople to go over these stale accounts and rank them in order of how much money they spent. You ask your salespeople to focus on the top 10 percent accounts in their territory and freshen up the point of contact. Then you tell them you are going to work together to create Mind Maps for their targets. You start by passing out spreadsheets with the following headings.

NEW CLIENT MIND MAPPING CHECKLIST

- Same contact
- New contact
- Years and months at position
- Promoted from within
- Outside hire
- New to state
- Former state of residence
- Former company
- Reason for leaving
- Family size

- New to job role
- Similar former position
- Previous title
- Gender affiliation
- Why they switched to your competitor

Have each rep make Mind Maps of their top 10 previous clients, starting with the biggest spender. Let's say your Florida rep's biggest spender had a changing of the guard. The new contact is Donna Kensington. Your rep puts the name Donna K in the center of the fresh piece of paper and makes a tight circle around her name. Referring to the spreadsheet, we see Donna is a recent hire for Made In the Shade Awnings (MITSA), which is Florida's top awning manufacturer and installer of customized awnings for household and commercial use. We also know Donna worked previously as a fractional HR/payroll provider for several businesses in Nebraska. She and her family made the move to Florida this past year.

We don't know why Donna would give up her own business to work for a midsized company in the South, but perhaps the idea of facing another Nebraska winter may have played a part. This is worth noting because it could spark some icebreaker small talk. Social media reveals that Donna has two daughters in middle school and a husband who works in heating and air-conditioning installation. Applying the model provided in Figure 9.1 may also provide some insights.

Looking at everything we now know about Donna, your rep can make some informed assumptions. The idea is for the rep to identify common ground for conversation and ways he or she might be helpful to the contact. For example, as a mom of two, Donna may need childcare support. Your rep can research the area's most highly rated schools, pediatricians, dental offices,

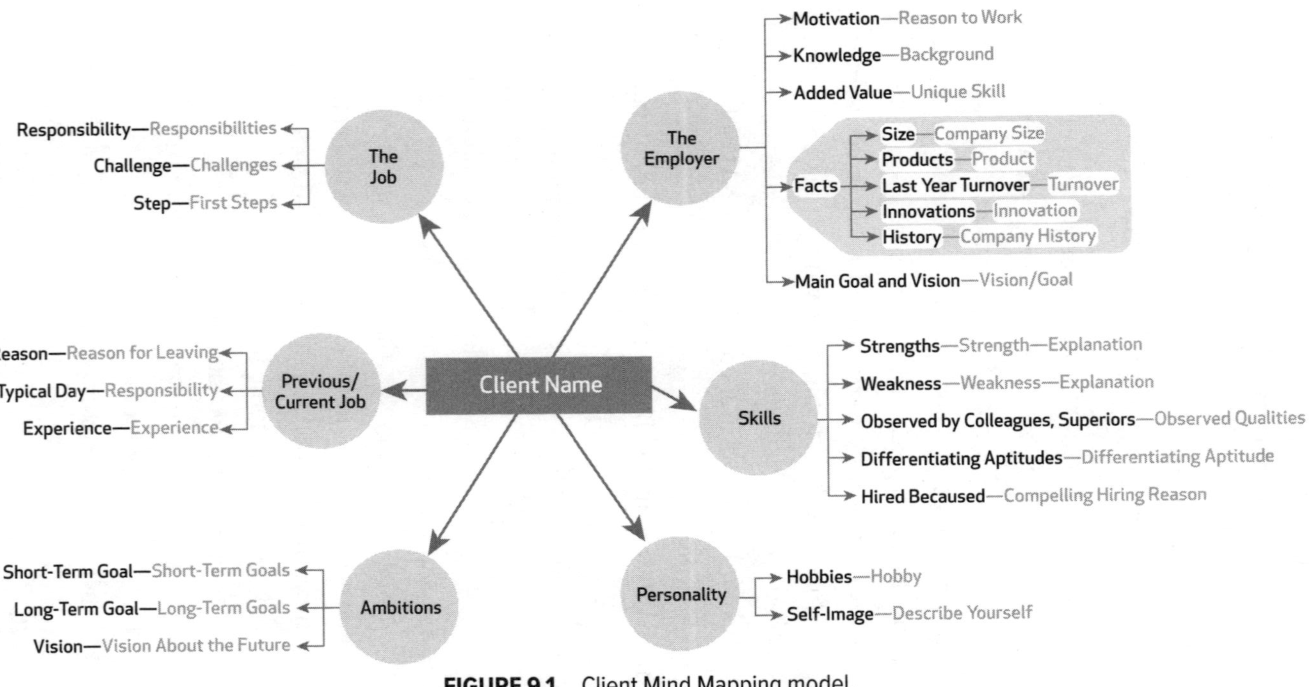

FIGURE 9.1 Client Mind Mapping model.

tutoring, summer camps, or organized sports. Since Donna is new to this company and the area, she will no doubt want to showcase her knowledge and build her network. She might appreciate a curated list of networking events and professional women's organizations in her area of Florida.

BONDING WITH STRANGERS

In the preceding example, you are giving your reps the tools to do something that challenges even the most seasoned businesspeople: bonding with strangers. Even the very best hostage negotiators, salespeople, leaders, managers, or entrepreneurs occasionally strike out during an initial encounter—especially if the meeting happens virtually. Here are a few tips that can make those first few meetings go more smoothly.

Stay Centered and Calm

Your voice and expressions have a strong influence on the other person's mood. Take a few moments to breathe deeply and collect yourself before an important call. Distill your main goal for the conversation. Define the place you'll calmly return to in your mind if stress starts to get the better of you. Never lose sight of your end goal, whether it's to improve a relationship, pitch an idea, or finalize the contract.

If your conversation includes sensitive matters—you're negotiating a contract, say, or holding an employee accountable—you may need to create a cooling-off period and suggest resuming the conversation later. When that's not possible, try shifting the conversation to another topic before returning to the contentious point. If conflict is unavoidable and immediate, respond with accommodating phrases that acknowledge the other person's point of view. Say things like, "You bring up some valid points." In addition to making someone feel heard, you're giving them space to breathe and time to think. As long as you keep cool, that can only benefit you.

Conduct Forensic Chitchat—or Don't

Pepper your small talk with open-ended questions. They can be about hobbies, celebrities, travel, old TV shows and movies . . . pretty much anything but religion or politics. It's a way to hear the person speak about what they love and who they admire. This can give you clues as to their deeply held beliefs and values. Is this a social justice person? Is this someone who's all about power? Is this person conventional or a maverick? Identifying shared values rapidly leads to a more intimate personal connection. Voice concise encouragement. Sprinkle in phrases like "That's right," or "I see what you mean," and then get out of the way.

Keep in mind that some people really are "all business" and yours is one of possibly many meetings scheduled that day, so respect their time. If they don't seem interested in small talk, quickly move on.

KEY TAKEAWAYS

- The Pattern of Life (POL) is a deep dive to understand someone who is going to have an ongoing impact on your business or career. The POL catalogs and analyzes a person's behaviors with the goal of understanding their attitudes, values, self-image, and aspirations.
- To conduct a POL assessment in a business setting, focus on the person's communication style, emails, what they do outside the office, and what they emphasize.
- Mind Mapping is a technique used to create a Personality Baseline of a person prior to your initial encounter. Find out what you can about the person's interests, family life, and work history. Then in the initial conversation, sprinkle in open-ended, casual questions and comments—unless the person signals they only want to discuss business.

CHAPTER 10

ADVANTAGE: YOU. UNDERSTANDING THE TWO TYPES OF CONVINCERS

As the human with the highest ever recorded IQ (228), the *Parade* magazine columnist Marilyn vos Savant is certainly no dummy. She said, "If your head tells you one thing and your heart tells you another, decide whether you have a better head or a better heart before you do anything." The head/heart dichotomy may seem trite, but when it comes to the art of convincing, she is on to something.

We believe there are two types of convincers: those who lead with emotion and those who lead with facts. It's essential to figure out whether your natural convincing style is emotional or fact based so you can calibrate your natural tendency to be too dramatic or, conversely, too dry. What's more, this works both ways. If you naturally lead with your head and bombard a heart type with studies and statistics, you'll find it challenging to engage them. On the other hand, if your default is to lead with your heart and overwhelm a head-type listener with over-the-top enthusiasm, you will not be taken seriously.

Now, let's say you and the person you are dealing with are both head types. They could appeal to your inner nerd and gain the upper hand by plying you with numbers and data. What if you're both heart people? They may be so good at selling their emotional argument they'll have your inner empath eating out of their hand. We've all felt like we are being baited, but some bait is so delicious, one overlooks the fact it is just an old piece of fish.

It's rare to find someone who is 50 percent head and 50 percent heart. In our experience, most people are around 70/30 percent one or the other. If you understand your own natural convincing style, you will set up your arguments differently to compensate and win more—especially if you also understand whether the person you are interacting with is more of a heart or a head type.

We all know people who clearly fall into the head or heart camp. The emotional convincer will ply you with personal anecdotes and examples, designed to make you feel something. The intellectual convincer will have memorized facts and figures and let the data do the talking. Let's take a closer look at these two types of convincers and their default techniques.

EMOTIONAL CONVINCER

This type of convincer uses truth laced with heavy emotion. Their story is powerful, but it could be laden with exaggeration and even untruths. Typically, emotional convincers lead from their own personal experience, which is hard to argue against. They have stories they use over and over to convince themselves and others that their point of view is correct.

A useful approach to understanding this type of convincer is to home in on the most exaggerated point in their story. This often reveals what they are trying to compensate or conceal.

For instance, Realtors study what would-be homeowners want and need in a new home and build an emotional connection to get the buyer to make an offer. When Bonnie, a Realtor, walked my friend Julie through her new house, Bonnie was super focused on how nicely the seller had upgraded the kitchen. The Realtor completely glossed over the two outdated bathrooms, which included 1980s wallpaper and bright blue and pink tile. The bathrooms would need to be torn out and upgraded, but the Realtor didn't even mention them. She instead focused on all the memories and special times the family would have in the open-concept kitchen. The Realtor was so gung-ho on selling the couple on the kitchen, she sent a follow-up thank-you note with an apple pie sitting on the counter in the sun-drenched kitchen. This was a flag that Bonnie didn't want the potential buyer to focus on the bathrooms, because it would bring the asking price down.

Too Personal, Too Soon: An Emotional Convincer's Use of TMI Backfires

We recently had a meeting with a prospective client whose behavior set off our Spidey-Sense. Before we could delve into his needs, wants, and business issues, the gentleman told us an extremely personal story—the kind most of us would only tell someone after we had known them a long time. He described a horrific car accident he had been in, complete with gory details that were undeniably true.

Our potential client confessed that he felt terrible guilt over the accident, which had forever colored his perspective on life. While he had not sustained any injuries, the crash left his friend paralyzed. As he told this story, likely for the hundredth time, our prospect became angry and emotional. The tale had nothing to do with the project he wanted us to work on, but he succeeded in hooking us. Just as we were about to break out the tissues, he suddenly switched gears and began negotiating the terms of our deal and eventual contract.

This is where we paused and asked for more time. Chip did some research and found another vendor who had worked with our prospect. When we told him the story and our gut reaction, he immediately said, "Stay away." Our potential client had used the same technique to drum up sympathy with this vendor.

While the technique of leading with his personal tragedy had likely worked for this man in the past, it was a little off-putting. We were so emotionally taken in by the story that the terms of the contract seemed almost fair. Fortunately, our respective backgrounds in PR and FBI investigations gave us both a nose for BS.

The story is meant to illustrate what to look for in someone who is trying to sway you in an unethical manner. Fortunately, most emotional convincers are not this dishonest. My mother is an extremely skilled emotional convincer. In my Italian American family, food is everything. I was a lucky girl. While other kids had sandwiches at lunchtime during school, I had garlicky eggplant parmesan. After my brother, sister, and I grew up and moved out, my mom took a job at Costco as a sample lady—hairnet and all.

One day, my mom was serving up chicken. Unimpressed with the bland samples, she went and bought an industrial-sized container of garlic salt to flavor her chicken. Her boss couldn't figure out why so many people bought garlic salt and chicken that day—they literally sold out. One by one, my mother told each customer how to spice things like an Italian grandma. People loved her stories. She told them she used the garlic salt in everything she cooked (except for dessert), and people bought the chicken and garlic salt in droves. She emotionally tied the customers to the purchase, and it worked.

FACT-BASED CONVINCERS

Fact-based convincers prime you with statistics and research to validate what they are about to say. They position themselves as unbiased arbiters of truth, though, of course, there is no guarantee they're not lying. They sometimes play both sides of an issue, presenting and then demolishing arguments against their point of view. This technique defuses your objections before you even have time to think them up. In the case of a data-driven person, the part of the data they claim is faulty can sometimes reveal what they are trying to conceal or compensate for.

It can be easy to spot this type of convincer because they are always citing new studies, research, or data to support their point of view or product. They tend to be analytical types who examine all the possible pitfalls of each decision—a useful mechanism to protect them from being proven wrong.

Here is a perfect example from a conversation Chip and I had with the author of *Accidental Genius*, Mark Levy.[1] He recounted the story of a keynote speaker who was totally wowing the audience at Content Marketing World until, in Mark's opinion, he made a fatal convincing error.

In an attempt to make a point about diversity, the speaker said, "Only tall white men ever get ahead in America. In fact, all US presidents have been over six feet tall." But Levy, who is a history buff, didn't buy it. He remembered James Madison and John Adams weren't that tall. His curiosity got the better of him. So with a few keystrokes on his phone, while the speaker continued, he entered: How tall was President James Madison? Mark's hunch was right. President Madison was only 5 foot 4, and he was in good company. Twenty-six other US presidents were under 6 feet. After learning this, Mark didn't want to listen to anything more the speaker had to say. His exaggerations made him lose all credibility.

An Emotional Sell: Pulling Heartstrings to Get the Board to Buy In

As leadership consultants based in Washington, DC, we do a lot of politically charged crisis communications work. The president of an association whose members are in the field of mental health came to us with an unusual problem. The association was planning their annual conference. They had picked a host city and were choosing hotels and caterers when a local politician passed a law enabling counselors to refuse to see patients whose lifestyles they disapproved of. This went against everything the association stood for.

The association president wanted us to help him convince his board of directors, made up of counselors from a variety of public and private practices, to move the conference in protest. The CEO got the board members on the phone and proceeded to explain how much the decision would cost. This included canceling the contract for the existing hotel and conference center as well as the cost of changing venues, hotels, and additional event-planning in a different city. The decision would cost the organization $1.2 million in the short term, plus several hundred thousand dollars down the line. The board was at a standstill and the clock was ticking. That's when we were called in.

When you are trying to convince a group, such as a board of directors, you should assume that it is made of both emotional and fact-based convincers. Our client had presented the numbers, assuming everyone on the board already believed moving the conference was "the right thing." But his fact-based argument to move the conference wasn't enough to get the buy-in.

We recommended sending out an association-wide survey to see how people felt about the new law and the decision to move the conference. When the CEO shared the results with his board, they decided to take a stand. The emotional convincers related to how their members felt about a law that allowed discrimination, and the fact-based convincers related to the results being presented in the form of a poll with clear results. This move garnered several awards and a cover story in the industry trade magazine. Our client was heralded as a hero for standing firm with the members' beliefs.

A Three-Step Formula to Get What You Want

The most-convincing people use either emotional or fact-based convincing techniques when they are trying to pitch an idea, service, or concept. Your best path to successfully convincing someone is:

1. Recognizing the other person's default convincing style
2. Predicting the other person's likely objections (What are their sticking points?)
3. Validating the other person's point of view within their default style (e.g., emotional: "Yes, you are right to feel excited about this." Or fact-based: "74 percent of people agree this is the right decision.")

Remember, no argument is ever so good that the person you are talking to throws up their hands and says, "You are right, I am 100 percent wrong." It never happens—even if we all fantasize about it. To be convincing, you must honor what the other person values.

The Call Back

Here's an example of some shrewd convincing using the Three-Step Formula. My friend Dara, a successful executive, was turning 40 and wanted to celebrate this milestone by buying a Mercedes convertible. She had an emotional connection to the brand and viewed that car as proof that she had "made it." Dara's husband, Drew, a lawyer specializing in financial fraud cases, was always reluctant to make large purchases, especially those he deemed extravagant. Dara had plenty of experience with her husband's approach to spending money, so she reworked her strategy to appeal to a fact-based convincer and turned the conversation into a laundry list of facts:

- Mercedes is rated one of the most reliable luxury cars on the market.
- Of all convertibles, Mercedes convertibles are the safest, with one of the best safety records to date.
- The car maintains its value longer than other brands in the luxury class of cars.

Then Dara went in for the kill. She addressed Drew's core objection head-on. "Drew," she cooed, with all the charm she could muster, "I know this is a bit of an extravagant purchase, just based on me liking Mercedes. But I think the research shows how this would be a sensible decision too."

You can see how the three-step formula factored in. But Dara added what we have named the Call Back. Not only did she use Drew's convincing style, but she also referenced her own emotional style from his point of view: "I know this might be an extravagant purchase." He felt heard, but he was also disarmed. They got the car.

THE PERSONALITY BASELINE: KNOW WHO YOU'RE DEALING WITH

As we said at the beginning of this chapter, most people favor one convincing style or the other. Few are equal parts head and heart, and few are on either extreme. Of course, human behavior is consistently inconsistent. We've all been surprised by people who say they will do one thing and do something else entirely. It's easy to get sucked into a conversation that is positioning you for failure. And while we can help you build a powerful convincing toolkit, none of us are perfect convincing machines.

Developing a Personality Baseline for the person you are dealing with can help you be more convincing and keep from getting manipulated. The Personality Baseline is how someone normally behaves and reacts. Finding out what drives someone's resistance can provide powerful insight into their baseline personality. As we are monitoring someone's behavioral patterns, we are determining how they think. Their baseline personality will let us know how we should build our argument. If they are resistant to emotional arguments, we will need more facts to convince them. Conversely, if they are more emotional, our approach needs to contain a human element.

In his FBI days, Chip watched many polygraph sessions. He even sat for a couple himself. A trained polygrapher will break up their question-and-answer session with a little small talk to relax and distract their subject. This provides a sense of how a person acts when asked questions they know the answers to. Questions start out as follows:

> Your name is ________________. True or False.
>
> You were born on ________________. True or False.
>
> You are from Delaware? True or False.
>
> I am going to make a statement and I am going to ask you to lie.
>
> You were born in New York, not Delaware. True or False.

That last question is a trick that reveals how their body reacts to lying. It helps the polygrapher spot deception in a subject's answers. Even polygraph experts get a baseline personality assessment through small talk, so you shouldn't ignore the importance of it in business. Small talk is anything but small. It can reveal a lot about someone and shouldn't be overlooked.

While we don't recommend asking a prospective client, employee, or business partner to take a polygraph, you can use your powers of observation to create a Personality Baseline profile for each person you interact with. Practice Forensic Listening after each of your initial encounters; write down some key things you noticed about them and how they want to be handled. As we've learned from recent political and legal scandals, FBI agents and attorneys are trained to take copious notes after verbal encounters, when the details and wording are fresh in their minds. Training yourself to be more observant of others will give you a distinct advantage over people who gloss over this type of detail.

How much of a baseline do you need? That depends on the prospective relationship. Watch the person in different situations. Your goal is to notice how they react under pressure:

- If you press them to answer a challenging question, do they answer emotionally or with facts, figures, and other types of "proof"?
- See if you can get them to tell you about their setbacks and successes. How do they describe what happened? How did they handle adversity? Are they quick to blame others?
- Are they buttering you up? And if so, are they good at it? (If you notice, it generally means they aren't!)
- How do they talk about themselves? Do they humblebrag? Are they downright boastful? Or are they more discreet and keep trying to turn the conversation back to you? Make note of what details about themselves they zero in on.
- Observe how they treat others, from the receptionist to the CEO.

Not every situation will expose a person's baseline, but seeing how they react in a variety of settings will give you a better sense of who they are.

Of course, a first impression is not enough to get a good baseline. Most of us are not totally authentic or relaxed when we first meet someone. You must observe someone in at least three to five settings before you can get a feel for their baseline personality. However, how a person acts the first time you meet them will give you a glimpse into what they are like under pressure.

According to a study that included 2,000 Americans, 7 in 10 people (69 percent) form a first impression of somebody before that person even speaks. It is up to you to observe the first meeting and record what you learn. Keep a file for important business relationships, and note key personality consistencies and inconsistencies.

Personality Consistencies and Inconsistencies

A Princeton University study found that people's Facebook "likes" can reveal their personality traits.[2] Social media companies can predict and model how users will behave on certain apps. While the way smartphone companies study our behavior often feels invasive, this type of behavioral modeling can uncover important information. That's why it's a good idea to learn how to do this type of modeling yourself, offline.

We define a Signature Personality Consistency as a behavior pattern someone displays in three or more different situations. The pattern signifies that the person is likely to act a certain way going forward. Studying the behavior of the people you interact with can make a difference in customer service, sales, negotiating a deal, and even in your personal life.

While this process seems relatively straightforward, remember, people are not always consistent from one situation to the next. Therefore, you need to examine Signature Personality Inconsistencies. People are consistently inconsistent, meaning their inconsistency shows up repeatedly, in the same ways. For example, a person who is nearly always calm and laid back but occasionally has a sudden meltdown over something trivial is demonstrating a Signature Personality Inconsistency. You must watch for these divergences from a person's norm and change your approach when they occur.

Getting to someone's personality takes time—even for FBI special agents.

THE FBI'S TWO CRITICAL QUESTIONS: WHAT IS THE SAME AND WHAT HAS CHANGED?

The timeline of an FBI investigation can vary greatly. Some investigations are wrapped up in two weeks, while others drag on for two years. As a case agent, Chip used to get frustrated when leads dried up and cases stalled.

For example, Chip was working on an investigation involving a builder who came forward claiming he was approached by a staffer for a politician's reelection campaign. The staffer allegedly demanded campaign contributions. Otherwise, the staffer threatened, his boss would see to it that all the builder's local building permits were pulled. The team decided to interview the target again to see what had changed—and what remained the same. This technique often leads to new insights that can bust a case wide open. To get a baseline, Chip and his team examined the following categories:

- **Stress.** How does the person behave under stress? Look at things like big projects, new responsibilities, or times when they are in the spotlight.
- **Happiness.** How do they respond to positive stimuli? Completion of a project, unexpected award, or accolade, signing a new client, and so on?

- **Anger.** What do they do when they are angry? Do they take responsibility for getting frustrated or blame others?
- **Irritation.** When they are irritated, do they isolate themselves or do they vent? If they complain, is it to a trusted confidant or to anyone who will listen?
- **Fear.** Do they panic easily? Go into "my way or the highway" mode? Do they get analysis paralysis? Are they too intimidated to make a decision or take action?
- **Disappointment.** Do they hold a grudge? Get angry or bitter? Blame others for their own failure?

Two Questions, One Answer

Josh, one of our coaching clients, was concerned he might lose a major source of revenue for his company. He had a feeling the client would not renew their contract and wanted us to help him figure out what was happening and how to save the relationship. We had already trained Josh in Forensic Listening and Forensic Note-Taking with his team and clients, so he wasn't just operating on instinct. He knew something was off.

Josh's client—let's call her Marie—ran a large division of an international bank. She was sounding increasingly anxious and edgy on the phone, and Josh couldn't figure out why. About three weeks before the annual renewal process, Marie stopped returning Josh's calls. When he finally managed to get through, she was evasive about the topic of future work. Josh was confused. Marie was normally very friendly and eager to discuss upcoming projects. He knew his company had been doing stellar work for Marie. He decided to call her to see if he could get confirmation on the deal. Instead of picking up his calls like she normally did, he was sent right to her voicemail.

We asked Josh if this had ever happened before. He said, "Yes, it happens every October, ever since we started working with them three years ago. But this year feels different—like Marie's anxiety is worse."

We asked our two critical questions:

1. What has changed?
2. What is the same?"

That's when Josh told us that Greg, a key account person at Josh's company, was often unavailable to discuss details about the accounts he managed. When Josh called, Greg was out sick or "in a meeting." When Josh finally got him on the phone, Greg sounded disengaged.

Josh was getting nervous and avoiding the situation out of fear. Not only is this a normal reaction, but as we discussed in Chapter 8, it is neurological. Dr. Judy Ho, a clinical and forensic neuropsychologist, says "self-sabotage lies in our biology."[3] Humans have two major drives to keep the species going: reproduction and self-preservation. When the instinct for self-preservation gets out of whack and becomes overactive, we experience fear in unnecessary places and situations, and because humans are social animals, that fear is often about social humiliation. We recognized that fear in Josh and helped him address his unconscious negative thoughts, regain some mental clarity, and confront the situation with Greg.

What was going on with Greg and Marie? Could there be a connection? Anyone who pays close attention to personality cues will tell you it's not as cut and dry as Marie being nervous. On the other hand, it would be difficult to argue that Marie wasn't acting differently. So where should Josh start?

We used our Two-Question Framework of Josh to get a picture for our analysis:

1. What Has Changed?

Marie's calls, emails, and texts had completely stopped. Josh noted that whenever Marie sent a request through Greg, she had no changes, additional asks, or complaints about the work. This felt out of character, as Marie was normally demanding and detail oriented.

As Josh reviewed how the dynamic had changed with Marie and Greg, he realized that Greg was increasingly a no-show at client status meetings, bailing out at the last minute with the excuse that he was being pulled into other projects. When we reviewed emails and phone calls, a pattern started to emerge:

- Last quarter, there had been 73 separate emails from Marie requesting changes. This quarter there were 12.
- Last quarter there were 48 phone calls and this quarter there were 2.
- Greg has become evasive and is almost never available for updates.

2. What Is the Same?

While Josh was understandably concerned about the upcoming renewal, there were no issues with his company's work, which was consistently on time, on target, and on budget. Other than Greg and Marie, the rest of the team's behavior toward Josh and his team had not changed.

Signature Personality Inconsistencies

Marie was displaying a Signature Personality Inconsistency, but considering her entire three-year business relationship with

Josh, this was not totally uncharacteristic. A pattern was beginning to emerge.

Looking back on his very first call with Marie, Josh remembered her bad-mouthing his predecessor. They needed too much oversight! There weren't enough senior people on her team! She had to do everything herself! Much as he wanted to keep the business, Josh admitted that Marie was a challenging client. She would try to increase Josh's workload to get more than she was willing to pay for. Rather than discuss differences in a mature manner, she would bully him to get her way. She just wanted the problem solved and off her plate and did whatever it took to burnish her own reputation. (This all-or-nothing attitude toward one's own success is one of the biggest red flags of potential unethical behavior.)

After a careful examination of his notes, emails, and texts, Josh decided it was time for a heart-to-heart with Greg. When confronted, Greg admitted that Marie had been recruiting him to go work for her.

The employee poaching Marie was attempting would result in Josh's company losing a significant amount of business. It had to stop. As soon as he understood what was going on, Josh took the issue to his company's human resources and legal team. He then went to Marie's immediate supervisor. Upon learning what Marie was doing, Marie's supervisor had her terminated for employee poaching. Josh's company got the renewal, and he strengthened his relationship with the customer.

IF YOUR DEFENSE IS AS GOOD AS YOUR OFFENSE, YOU WIN

What you have learned in this chapter should do more than help you be more convincing: it can also help protect you from getting played by a worthy adversary. But beware! As convincing as this framework is, the strategy we are providing doesn't guarantee you will win every single time. There will be misunderstandings and glitches, and you will make mistakes. It's like when you dictate a text that says, "I will meet you for lunch at 2 p.m.," and autocorrect turns it into, "Let's do brunch and not invite Kim." Your friend still knows that you want to have lunch with her, which is the point. Even if you don't achieve perfection in every conversation, you will be far ahead of where you started.

KEY TAKEAWAYS

- There are two types of convincers: those who lead with emotion and those who lead with facts. It's essential to figure out whether your natural convincing style is emotional or fact-based, so you can calibrate your natural tendency to be too dramatic or, conversely, too dry. The emotional convincer will ply you with personal anecdotes and examples, designed to make you feel something. The intellectual convincer will have memorized facts and figures and let the data do the talking.
- Your best path to successfully convincing someone is to recognize the other person's default convincing style, predict the other person's likely objections (What are their sticking points?), and validate the other person's point of view within their default style.
- Develop a Personality Baseline for the person you are dealing to help you be more convincing and keep

from getting manipulated. The Personality Baseline is how someone normally behaves and reacts.

- A Signature Personality Consistency is a behavior pattern someone displays in three or more different situations. The pattern signifies that the person is likely to act a certain way going forward.
- Two-Question Framework is an FBI investigatory technique that involves looking at a situation in terms of what has changed and what has stayed the same.

CHAPTER 11

CONCERT CONVINCING

Power can be a weakness. Taking the stage at the United Nations in New York City was a pivotal moment in my career. I was asked to speak about utilizing influence to create change to more than 500 international diplomats.

While I was so proud to contribute to the United Nations' sustainable development goals to create a safer, better world, it all came crashing down at lunch. The cafeteria at the United Nations was so badly organized, I probably couldn't even get a banana without waiting in an hour-long line. I thought to myself, "How are they going to solve the world's problems if I can't even get a piece of fruit?"

Then I realized that there were probably a lot of people involved with trying to make this cafeteria work, probably too many people. I would say that the United Nations is one of those organizations where its power is also its weakness. While it's got the power of all these voices, it's also got the weakness of all those voices. Too many to make change work and work quickly.

As a crisis communications professional for the past 20 years, I can tell you convincing groups of people can be a challenge. While knowing a group's "collective belief" can certainly make you more convincing, you must first understand the group's shared experience. How do they view the world? What does the group believe is true, and what do they believe is not true? Asking these questions and validating the group's beliefs is an effective persuasive technique, also known as Concert Convincing.

When I spoke at the United Nations, many people working for non-government organizations (NGOs) had incredible missions. They were part of citizen groups organized on a local, national, or international level to address issues in support of the public good. From helping widows in war-torn countries to preventing children from being exploited in India's massive trash heaps, these people were desperate to get the word out about their causes. They asked me, "How do I get people to care about what we are doing?" The first thing I recommended was to understand what the people they were targeting believed to be true:

- Who is the current authority on this topic that the group looks up to or respects?
- What aspect of the cause would everyone like to back?
- How many people are being affected? Do they have testimonials from several people who can talk about the mission?
- Why do people "pretend" this is or isn't happening?
- What is the uncomfortable truth they are denying?
- How do you bring these beliefs (right or wrong) to life without alienating people?

WHY FOUNDATIONAL KNOWLEDGE IS KEY

The reason people believe things are one way or another is they were taught how to view the world when they were young. When you were told what to believe before age seven by someone you trust, it becomes an almost unshakable truth and a part of your core belief system.

The reason someone is persuasive or not persuasive is usually based on a foundational belief. For instance, people who grew up with a parent who told them, "Don't ask questions when you first meet someone, because it is impolite," will likely not be able to learn enough about people up front. Therefore, it will be difficult for them to be convincing.

As we've described in previous chapters, one of the best ways to be convincing is to learn what the other people believe to be true. In this case, it is what the group thinks is true.

Have a plan of what you want the group to do, think, and feel as a result of your argument. Factor in the various personalities in the group. Are they emotional or fact-based? If persuasion is your goal, you need to plan for three components: thoughts, feelings, and actions. Dr. Robert Bontempo, a behavioral scientist and professor at Columbia University, says it comes down to three things:

1. What do I want them to think?
2. What do I want them to feel?
3. What do I want them to do?

What Do They Want to Think, Feel, and Do?

When the Infectious Disease Society of America (IDSA) called us in, they were experiencing some negative feedback from patients who were diagnosed with Lyme disease. The Society's new guidelines, which it was about to release, would impact patient care. In the past, every time the guidelines were updated, options for doctor visits, medicine, and treatments changed and people became livid. This prompted us to figure out what the public could agree on.

We landed on funding. Everyone, including IDSA, doctors, and patients, all wanted better funding for research into the causes and treatment of Lyme disease. We asked patients to join us in signing online petitions asking medical entities to address the disease and its effects. Additionally, we interviewed and surveyed patients, doctors, and practitioners. IDSA used a dedicated page to report on what it learned about the issue. Now, was everyone convinced? No. But a large majority of patients felt they had a clearer direction on how to think, feel, and what to do about their diagnosis.

This was the three-step formula at work for convincing a group:

1. What do I want them to think? IDSA wanted patients to realize they care about the well-being of patients.
2. What do I want them to feel? IDSA wanted patients to feel better and support research.
3. What do I want them to do? The organization wanted patients to ask for better medical research.

A Multimillion-Dollar Convincing Strategy

Now imagine trying to get a group of delivery drivers—who had been successful at their jobs—to adopt a new technology. That is exactly what Jack Levis was up against.

As a UPS employee, Levis led the development of ORION, an optimized routing system that's transformed how UPS drivers do their jobs. He developed a routing system that uses high-level math to determine the most efficient delivery route for every driver. The project was extraordinarily successful, cutting 100 million miles of driving every year by UPS and its drivers. But this didn't happen overnight.

We sat down with Levis to interview him for this book: "Innovation doesn't just take a great idea. It requires a lot of patience and thick skin," said Levis. He fundamentally challenged the status quo that had been in place for more than 90 years. "This system changed what the drivers believed to be the quickest way to deliver packages," said Levis.[1]

Over the course of four years, he gathered all the predictive data he could find, created prototypes, and got the attention and support of a senior executive at the company who helped him champion the project. The innovation made drivers think, feel, and do deliveries differently.

This framework is effective because it is simple. Even the most complex ideas must hit on these three fundamental truths to convince a group.

Your Foundational Beliefs as the Convincer

You must reexamine what you really believe. Not what you think, not what you hope, not what someone said you should believe, but what you really believe to be true. Everyone wants to think they have the power to influence people. However, trying something new is very risky for adults. Most of us don't try new things unless external forces are at play. Years ago, I was working for a boss who tried to keep me down by telling me that what she had achieved was completely out of reach for me. She wanted me to believe other people felt this way about my potential too. She even said clients didn't think I had "what it took" either. But she revealed her manipulative tactic when she knew that I single-handedly won a $350,000 account for her agency.

To "motivate" me, she took me to the mansion she was building for her family. "Look around," she said, "I could never have built this house without the work you contributed to my company. Just remember, you still have a long way to go before you could ever get to my level of success."

I didn't realize it immediately, but I took what she said as a challenge. In that moment, she had accidently convinced me to be my own boss. Shortly after, I started my own business and have been an entrepreneur for the past 17 years. When I've gone toe-to-toe with my old boss, competing for the same accounts, I have won every time.

Has that ever happened to you? Have you ever had someone challenge you based on a wrongly held belief about your potential? Although my boss didn't mean to convince me that way—I truly believed I was capable of more—she just didn't know it. She didn't have the same view of me that I had of myself. This dissonance motivated me to prove her wrong.

How Wrongly Held Beliefs in Your Industry Can Help You Start a Trend

Trends give people clues to decipher emerging needs, shifts, opportunity, and changes in customer behavior or beliefs. Every leader needs to evaluate if they have the right products and services. That's why predicting trends is so powerful—if you are the one to do it.

Simply put, developing trends is a secret weapon for leaders to stand out. Put together information from three different but credible sources, come to a conclusion about those facts, and claim your interpretation as what you see coming around the corner. Basically, you tell people what to do, think, and feel based on what you see happening in your industry. This will help position you as an expert in trade and business media.

CREATE A TREND IN THREE STEPS

Developing trends for our clients is one of our secrets to successfully positioning thought leaders in any field. Here are several frameworks to begin thinking about creating your industry trend.

Step 1. What Do People in Your Industry Think Is True?

As an industry insider in any field, you probably have a pretty good feel for what people in your industry believe is an established truth. If you don't know, look at industry trade publications. For instance, if you are a restaurateur, read *Restaurant Week* and study what others are saying right now.

Step 2. How Do You Want People to Feel About This Trend?

Look for sources to back up your idea. Find data and research to support your trend idea from respected and credible publications and authorities. This could include other thought leaders in your field, university professors, *Harvard Business Review*, or other published scholarly works. For the best results, look for research that has been created within the past two years.

Step 3. What Do You Want People to Do as a Result of Your Trend?

Explain why people should also see the same pattern you see. Based on what you come up with, you want to name the trend something clever, creative, and repeatable. Think about recent trends that everyone now knows: the Great Resignation, Work from Home (WFM), Zoom Fatigue, and so on. Someone somewhere came up with these trends, found supporting data, named them, and claims them.

Joe Pulizzi and the Content Marketing Trend

However, this is where most people fall short in the way of Concert Convincing. They fail to promote themselves once the idea takes hold. That was not the case for the founder of Content Marketing World, Joe Pulizzi.

We talked with Pulizzi, who recently sold the event he launched and grew for more than $17.6 million dollars. He told us he had been trying to sell printed magazines to chief marketing officers, with little success. Pulizzi did what any good marketer does and started asking his customers what they needed help with. He thought, "all of these brands need to become their own media companies."[2] So he asked CMOs, and they all agreed that was something they were struggling to figure out. Then he came up with the term "content marketing" and started talking about the content marketing trend, and people were intrigued. Once the trend started to take off, he thought he could help more people by holding a conference—it sold out. The event grew bigger every year. Pulizzi put himself in the middle of a trend he created and built a successful business around it. Here's how you can too.

PLUG-AND-PLAY TREND FRAMEWORKS

To give you a head start, we have developed an easy plug-and-play trend framework, which we call the Back to the Future Framework. Don't get too caught up in being right or wrong about your trend. Most members of the media are looking for smart, credible people with authority and a point of view.

Besides, no one ever goes back to last year's trend reports to see if they were correct in the predictions. Simply making a prediction will make you someone others want to interview and listen to.

This is a three-part framework. It shows how things are evolving over time, what they look like now, and how they will most likely look in the future. Here's an example:

Part 1: In the Past

Most companies and leaders had a top-down leadership approach to leading employees.

Part 2: Now

With the emergence of Work from Home, employees are experiencing record levels of burnout, and we think we know why: (This is where you plug in smart research from three different credible sources to prove your point.)

- Three in five (59%) employees and business leaders say their organization has taken at least some measures to guard against burnout, according to a recent survey by The Workforce Institute at UKG and Workplace Intelligence.[3]
- U.S. Bureau of Labor Statistics announced that 4.3 million Americans, or 2.9 percent of the entire workforce, quit their jobs.[4]
- The Great Resignation is real, and it can be seen across virtually all industries.

Part 3: In the Future

Leaders will have to offer more counseling and mental health options to ensure employees' needs are being met. We call this the needs-first trend. (This is where you insert your prediction and name the trend.)

HOW TO APPLY THE BACK TO THE FUTURE FRAMEWORK

IN THE PAST

Describe an established way of doing business.

For example:

Over the past few years shopping online has gotten easier than ever before.

NOW

Describe how the marketplace is beginning to change and the new trend that is emerging.

For example:

Consumer technology has become much easier to navigate than work technology. Increasingly, people are going to want to join companies that make work as easy as everyday living.

Provide data/research that supports your assertion:

- Baby boomers leaving the workforce in droves, and the job market is making it harder for companies to recruit and retain talent.
- Companies are looking for new ways to stand out to job candidates.

IN THE FUTURE

Insert your prediction and name the trend.

For example:

Business technology will become much easier for employees. It will become like ordering products on Amazon. We call this the Consumer Business Tech Trend.

HOW TO USE THE BACK TO THE FUTURE FRAMEWORK

The trends you identify using the Back to the Future Framework can be used in so many ways, including trend reports, sound bites for media interviews, topics for speaking engagements, and media pitches to obtain placements.

KEY TAKEAWAYS

- Trends give people clues to decipher emerging needs, shifts, opportunity, and changes in customer behavior or beliefs. Every leader needs to evaluate if they have the right products and services. That's why predicting trends is so powerful—particularly if you are the one to do it. Simply put, identifying trends is a secret weapon for leaders to stand out from the crowd.
- There are several frameworks for identifying trends. The Back to the Future Framework that we developed relies on understanding established business practices, the dynamics of change in today's markets, and what those changes portend for the future.

CHAPTER 12

CONVINCING TACTICS AND NEGOTIATION

If a hostage taker is going to agree to negotiate, he must believe his life matters as much to the negotiator as the lives of his captives. It sounds like a tall order, but criminals are wired a little differently than the rest of us and that can work to the law's advantage, especially when "the law" is a highly trained FBI agent. The first thing Chip needed to do in these situations was to convince the hostage taker that Chip had the hostage taker's best interest in mind.

As Chip puts it, "There is no 'win-win scenario' in a hostage situation. No BATNA (best alternative to a negotiated agreement). I wasn't about to say, 'Hey, you've got seven people. Give me back four, kill three, and we will call it a day.' I had to convince, not negotiate with, the hostage taker. My job was to get him to value what I valued—the safety of everyone involved. I had to appeal to his interests, not to reason. My professional objective was to protect *everyone's* safety, even that of the hostage taker."

With most of his law enforcement career spent coaxing targets on analog phone lines, high-definition video calls are a luxury. Chip says, "For me it's almost information overload," he says. "It's like a fire hose of vibrancy and color!" Video calls are great leverage for negotiations because you can learn so much about a person's relationship to money by observing their home and asking a few questions about their background.

In business conversations, especially negotiations, Chip tries to start with small talk filled with questions to uncover people's history with money. We might use recent events that show how a company grew or invested money and ask what they thought about that strategy. "Did you hear about the merger between these two companies? What do you think of their growth style?"

Or the questions could be about hobbies. Do they gravitate toward sports like sailing, tennis, and crew? Or are they more into crafts and cooking, with an emphasis on staying close to home? If you get them to tell you about their latest vacation, the details will say a lot about what they value. Did they take a first-class flight, opt for business class, or settle for coach? When you ask them about their vacation, how do they talk about where they stayed and the experience they had? Is it about the experience or the discount on the resort? This is a way to hear the person speak about what they value, which by proxy, can communicate their deeply held beliefs about money. You may be able to factor some of what you've learned into the negotiation to communicate the value of working with you or your organization.

THE PERCEPTION OF GETTING A GOOD DEAL

We were negotiating with a financial institution on a high-profile training program to help internal investigators spot fraud. Knowing that the person we were negotiating with would have to pitch the training services to the internal procurement office for approval, we set up our pricing to reflect how she would sell it up to her supervisors. We know people in finance are largely driven by "getting a good deal." That is why we set up our pricing structure three ways:

1. The lowest profitable price point
2. The middlemost profitable price point
3. The highest profitable price point

In the proposal and the negotiations, each price was justified with services provided as well as risk the client would have to assume with each option. The lowest price point made the client assume the most risk. The middle made us assume a little more risk than they did. Finally, with the highest price point we assumed the most risk, but also offered the biggest discount. During the negotiations, we spoke to directly to the procurement officer over a video call.

Naturally, we used the strategy mentioned previously and asked our negotiating partner where he vacationed. He mentioned he goes to Tuscany every year with his large Italian family. He revealed that there was always more food than anyone could ever eat, and he hated to throw away food. This revealed that he had a good relationship with money but wanted to ensure not to waste any of it. We had what we needed.

As the negotiations progressed, he asked, "I am curious how you came to this price." That's when we highlighted the value of the price and what he was to gain based on the risk involved. He said, "That makes a lot of sense." The procurement officer waited three business days before a response and opted for the highest price point.

HOW HOSTAGE NEGOTIATION APPLIES TO BUSINESS NEGOTIATION

Chip's transition from the FBI to being an entrepreneur made it clear that everything he learned as a hostage negotiator was applicable to both business and life. While lives may not be at stake in business, making people feel you have their best interest in mind will set you apart. It is something most of us don't consider, especially in professional settings. Ultimately, you cannot control what another person is going to do. What you can do is positively influence their behavior and decisions using the frameworks we offer in this book.

Another important takeaway from life in the bureau is to always look for a more creative outcome. Sometimes sticking to your guns leads to shooting yourself in the foot. For example, let's say a chief revenue officer (CRO) of a hair care company—we'll call it Hair & Now—wants to purchase another shampoo company, which she believes will add value to their existing product line.

The CEO and the board of directors find this company too expensive and see more risk than potential upside. Both sides are dug into their positions. The result is dysfunctional board meetings, full of resentment and acrimony. A trained negotiator will seek to bring people to a more rational mindset, by saying the following:

- We can all agree that we need to do something different to attract this important and growing part of our customer base.
- How else can we attract this sector of the market quickly? A merger and acquisition is expensive and a bit riskier than other business moves we've made in the past.
- What is in our power today to stop our competitors, who are grabbing companies, from getting our market share and taking our customers?

An expert intermediary would start by asking the CRO why she believes the potential acquisition will add more value to Hair & Now. This line of questioning reveals that the company the CRO is targeting has an avid tween following on social media. That would be an ideal complement to Hair & Now's current product line, which has not attracted a young audience despite aggressive marketing. The CRO feels this purchase would give the company the cachet it needs to be relevant in this growing market segment.

Now there's an understanding of the reasoning behind the CRO's request. Not only does this defuse the tension between the board and the CRO, but it also opens up a whole new array of possibilities. What about developing an offsite product/brand accelerator within Hair & Now to target this market segment? Perhaps the competitor's brand marketer might be interested in a new challenge. As in a hostage situation, sometimes finding creative solutions to a problem just takes asking the right questions. However, nothing beats a team-based approach.

NEGOTIATION IS A TEAM SPORT

The late entrepreneur and spokesman for Remington, Victor Kiam, once said, "A negotiator should observe everything. You must be part Sherlock Holmes, part Sigmund Freud."[1] We believe Kiam had it right. So many things happen during a negotiation, such as:

- Developing a relationship with the other party
- Figuring out what matters to them and what they value most
- Power dynamics
- Reading the other person's body positioning and the pitch, tone, and cadence of their voice
- Regulating your own body positioning and voice so as to appear friendly and open while giving nothing away
- Understanding how much money is available
- Thinking of a possible and agreeable future that will please the buyer

Negotiations are dynamic and hard for a single person to do effectively. That's why we believe negotiations are a team sport.

THERE'S NO SUCH THING AS THE PERFECT MULTITASKER

Our culture glamorizes multitasking, but as millions of people can attest, something always has to give. If we examine the negatives of multitasking through the Dunning-Kruger effect, we come to understand why.

We go through our personal and private lives with an endless to-do list, and every time we check something off, we like to think we accomplished it to the best of our abilities. Yet according to research conducted by David Dunning and Justin Kruger from Cornell University, people tend to overrate their own abilities.[2] Your brain simply won't allow you to assess whether you're turning your negotiating partner off or doing a stellar job. Overestimating your own abilities will not only affect your decision-making, but it may also even stop you from changing your approach. This isn't just a nice theory we have—it's been proven with neurological research.

Research by Dr. René Marois, published in the journal *Neuron*, shows that portions of the brain act as information bottlenecks, which results in "clogging information transfer from one portion of the brain to another. The results from this study indicated the primary bottleneck occurred when the lateral frontal, superior frontal, and prefrontal cortices had difficulties processing two tasks simultaneously."[3] Rather, a "queuing" of the tasks occurred so that the brain could process them individually and sequentially. What's interesting is the idea that, as Marois notes, "if tasks were presented with a delay of one second or more between, the bottlenecking effect was eliminated."

In negotiations, when you pause to figure out what to do next, you stop paying attention to what is happening in the room or on your computer screen. That means you are missing critical information. You can avoid this by clearly assigning roles for the presentation in advance so your negotiating partner or team can compensate for what you will inevitably miss, and vice versa. You know yourself and you know what you are likely to focus on. Delegate the other tasks.

WHY A TEAM-BASED NEGOTIATION WORKS BEST

If you can put together an experienced negotiation team, we highly recommend it. Negotiation is fast, and persuasion is slow.

Marois breaks down the differences between the two processes. Negotiations have clearly assigned roles and desired outcomes and can often be completed in a few hours. Changing someone's belief system takes time. Table 12.1 displays the difference between the two techniques.

TABLE 12.1 Negotiation Versus Convincing

Negotiation	Convincing
Fast	Slow
Doing	Believing
Start off with an opening they will reject	Start off with the latitude of agreement
You should go first	They should go first
Expensive	Free
Overt	Subtle

At every negotiation, you must wear multiple hats. Here's a list of roles for negotiations that we recommend as a minimum for important deals:

- **Speaker.** As the speaker you must control the dialogue. The skilled negotiator controls the conversation without appearing to do so. Being a speaker is a daunting role in a negotiation.
- **Decision maker.** The second most important role is the decision maker. Am I going to counter? Am I going to walk away? Am I going to escalate and de-escalate?

Whereas speaking is a behavioral process, decision-making is a cognitive process.

- **Behavioral analyst.** Try to bring along an observant person to serve as the behavioral analyst. They are monitoring the emotions and behaviors of the different parties and reviewing how the other party is reacting to your points and suggestions. They are also thinking about whether the behavior is consistent with what has been in past conversations.

In summary, the speaker is controlling the dialogue, the decision maker is processing all the information, and the behavioral analyst is processing emotions. To think one person can do all these roles on their own is unrealistic.

ACHIEVE SUPERIOR OUTCOMES

Understanding how to put together a team that works well together under extreme circumstances is critical in any business situation. Closing a sale, handling a merger, selling your company, trying to convince investors to take a chance on you, or just reacting to your shareholders and what your board is saying can feel like you're going through a crisis. Assembling the team we just described can work to your advantage to achieve superior outcomes.

In addition to the speaker, decision maker, and behavioral analyst, there is one more role that is often overlooked—what Professor Bontempo calls the back channel. "It is well-known that in Japanese cultures the decision maker is never in the room," says Bontempo. "They use this as a smart tactic to remain in control and offer themselves mitigation if the negotiation comes to a standstill. This is called the *Wizard of Oz* Technique. No one gets to see the great and powerful Oz. Essentially, this is a way to say, 'Thank you, I've heard what you said, now, we will see what the decision maker says.'"

While we may not have put a name to it, most of us have used the *Wizard of Oz* Technique in business when putting off a decision, deferring the responsibility to the CEO, board of directors, or legal. Having someone in reserve when there are bad feelings, ultimatums, or drama is a good way to keep the negotiation going in a civil but strategic way.

WHY A CRISIS IS A PERSUADER'S BEST FRIEND

Hostage negotiation is a life-or-death crisis, both for the criminal himself and the person trying to talk him out of doing something rash. As summarized in the title of a popular book, the hostage negotiator is *Stalling for Time*. The stalling process here is not really a negotiation: it is an exercise in convincing.[4] A hostage negotiation is a crisis. And crisis is a persuader's best friend.

Now you may not be dealing with life or death, but as Chip likes to say, "Stress is relative."

Crisis is a persuader's best opportunity to move people down the Convincing Continuum. During a business crisis, people are more likely to pay attention and change their minds because the crisis is a moment in time when their previously held beliefs are no longer serving them well.

Just consider the Covid-19 pandemic and consumer adoption of new technologies. Suddenly, we were willing to download apps, grocery shop from home, get contactless food delivery, and wear masks. In a matter of weeks, people adopted entirely new belief systems about what they would and wouldn't be willing to do in the "new normal."

CREATING A CRISIS TEAM

Let's dive into the FBI Hostage Rescue Team and see what roles might make sense for readers to emulate in high-stress business situations.

As you might suspect, there's a big difference between FBI reality and TV FBI reality—which is one of Chip's favorite things to gripe about. As he likes to point out, "Crime dramas are grounded in many of the stereotypes from the old days of law enforcement. This is also true of movies and shows involving hostage events. Invariably the hostage negotiator is a hard-nosed, tough-talking, take-no-prisoners kind of personality, who is going toe-to-toe in a verbal battle with the hostage taker."

In reality, the FBI takes a team-based approach to all the agency's crisis negotiations, and empathy is the most used weapon in the hostage negotiator's arsenal. The hostage team consists of a coach, lead investigator, intel, team leader, and liaison. The hostage negotiator is the only person communicating with the hostage taker. The rest of the team is silent, but definitely not static.

On-Scene Commander

The on-scene commander oversees the overall operation and is always in the loop for big decisions. He is communicating in real time with other officials. In corporate America, his equivalent would be the CEO.

Coach

The role of the coach is to sit right next to the hostage negotiator and monitor their mental and physical well-being. The coach's duties include:

- Providing support and encouragement to the negotiator through notes and nonverbal gestures—especially welcome during a long, grueling negotiation
- Serving as another set of ears for the hostage negotiator
- Acting as an emotional check to make sure the negotiator doesn't get pulled into reacting rather than responding with trained and measured techniques
- Vetting all the other team members' ideas, passed to the coach in notes

In corporate America, the coach is someone from the C-suite and could be a vice president, director, or other executive in charge of maintaining corporate morale.

Team Leader

The team leader works with the commander to coordinate the mission. They ensure that the group is working as a cohesive unit, monitor everyone's output and emotions, keep and check logs, and update the team as needed. In a business context, this could be anyone from the CFO to a high-ranking member of the human resources department.

Investigator

Tasked by the team leader, the investigator runs down leads and other points of investigative interest pertaining to the situation at hand. They also determine what information is worth disseminating to the rest of the team. In the business world, this would likely be someone with a crisis communications background.

Intel

This person's job is to record and categorize the information that is coming in from the live hostage situation. This is done under three headings:

1. **Danger.** This could be anything that could be used to harm people, like a gun, knife, or bomb.
2. **Positive information.** This involves any details that the subject (hostage taker) might respond to in a positive way, such as a beloved family member or favorite sport or hobby.
3. **Pedigree.** This is typically biographical information, such as name, age, where they grew up, whether they have been in trouble with the law before, if they have a gun license, and so on.

Liaison

This is the person tasked with managing communication between the on-scene commander and the SWAT team.

The reason this team is set up this way is to ensure the best possible outcome, with everyone focusing on their specialty. In optimum situations, the hostage negotiation is done on speakerphone so the whole team can hear and evaluate the conversation—unlike what happens in business.

The bureau recommends a team of six, so we don't think it is outrageous for us to suggest you bring at least one other person to a live negotiation. Negotiation is a team sport, even if you're just a team of two, but the roles and chemistry must be worked out in advance.

MONEY, EMOTIONS, AND WHAT OTHERS VALUE IN A NEGOTIATION

Some business leaders contend that emotions have no place in negotiations. To this Chip responds, "OK, so machines are going to be doing the negotiating?" People who believe they can keep emotions out of a business deal are deluding themselves. This is a dangerous belief that also deprives them of a powerful tool. If you know what you are doing, understanding and harnessing emotions can help you convince others and achieve your aims.

Ebb and Flow of a Negotiation

The FBI team has a coach to keep the negotiator's spirits up. Even if you can bring only one other person to the table, your associate can help support you if things are not going your way.

The two of you must decide your bending or breaking points in advance and be willing to walk away if those terms aren't met. The second person should be focused on both your preferred outcome and the other party's best interest.

What If I Don't Have Two People?

If your exchange is via phone or Zoom, ask permission to record so that someone with Forensic Listening ability can assess the conversation after the fact, looking for patterns and for emotional clues.

Advantage of a Two-Person Post-Review

This can work in your favor, especially if you are negotiating with a person who is exceptionally guarded. Because your colleague is there to listen and observe, they will be better able to objectively look at the conversation and assess body language, repetition, themes, pauses, and so on.

What If You Don't Have a Lot of Negotiation Experience?

Inexperienced negotiators often bargain with themselves before the negotiation even begins. They devalue their services and make their pricing as low as possible, leaving little wiggle room. When we are advising these clients, we always walk them through the three-tiered bracketing method described earlier in this chapter. Start with what you estimate the bid should be and the highest number you've been paid for your services in the past.

KEY TAKEAWAYS

- Empathy is the most used weapon in the hostage negotiator's arsenal because it helps them create a connection with the hostage taker. While lives may not be at stake in business, striving to understand others and making people feel you have their best interest in mind will set you apart from others in many business situations.
- In negotiations, when you pause to figure out what to do next, you stop paying attention to what is happening in the room or on your computer screen. That means you are missing critical information. You can avoid this by clearly assigning roles for the presentation in advance so your negotiating partner or team can compensate for what you will inevitably miss.

- For important deals, we recommend having a minimum of three people assigned to the negotiation: a speaker who controls the dialogue, a decision maker who determines what's an acceptable deal, and a behavioral analyst who monitors the emotions, behaviors, and reactions of the different parties, as well as assesses whether their behavior is consistent with past conversations. If you can't get a team of three together, at least bring one person with you. Decide on your roles in advance. If you must negotiate solo, Zoom is a great tool. Ask permission to record, and use Forensic Listening later to analyze the conversation.
- Crisis is a persuader's best opportunity because the crisis is a moment when people's previously held beliefs no longer serve them well.

CHAPTER 13

HOW TO BECOME A NATURAL NEGOTIATOR

Some people are born with perfect pitch. Some have exceptional athletic ability, artistic talent, or an ear for languages. And some are natural negotiators. Yes, that is "a thing," and the best negotiators are indeed naturals.

Blessed with the trifecta of qualities described in the following section, the Natural Negotiator is difficult to beat. But while it's not possible to teach a tone-deaf person to sing like Luciano Pavarotti, the skills that make a Natural Negotiator can be taught.

What makes a Natural Negotiator?

CONCENTRATION AND CLARITY

Laser-focused on their objective, Natural Negotiators express themselves with simple eloquence and clarity, and their communication style feels completely natural to others. They dial in to one person at a time. When you're talking, they seem to hang on your every word. When they're talking to you, you feel like the only person in the room. It's obvious that they're listening closely. And when you respond, they manage to find a nugget of common ground in anything you say, even when you fundamentally disagree.

FREE OF WORRY AND DOUBT

However high the stakes or tense the atmosphere, Natural Negotiators maintain a calm, even demeanor. They don't let worry and doubt get in the way of their performance or their objective. If somebody thinks you're doubting them, they start to justify their behavior. A Natural Negotiator will never put you on the defensive that way.

A PASSION FOR HELPING OTHERS

Natural Negotiators are driven by their desire to help others achieve their goals. Their positivity is infectious, and their can-do spirit leads people to believe that however far apart both parties are in the negotiation, an agreement can eventually be reached.

Chip is a Natural Negotiator. Not many of us could convince a dangerous sociopath that we care what happens to him.

Chip can and has. And he's saved his share of innocent people in the process. How did he do it? Chip says:

> If I'm focusing on someone, I'm looking at them, and I'm making eye contact. I'm concentrating on what they're saying. I'm not trying to put on airs or impress them with fancy language. Instead, I'm being very plainspoken on purpose, and they get it. If I don't seem worried, that lack of worry and doubt can be contagious. The negotiation grows more successful as people pick up on my passion for helping others. If you want to ease someone into a state of clarity and concentration, free of worry and doubt, you must lead by example—you show up in that state.

Every executive education course, MBA program, and business college curriculum has as a central core offering on negotiation. They promise to help you *get to a yes*, find your BATNA, and experience a win-win. However, these concepts all have their shortcomings, as even their most ardent proponents will agree.

These negotiation staples teach structure, theory, and process, but they are not designed as templates you can easily apply in the rough and tumble world of real business settings. Classes take you through case studies and practical exercises to uncover different styles and determine whether certain practices were applied. The ideas will be comprehensive, the arguments sound, the methods . . . forgettable. You know in your gut there is more to negotiation than what they teach you in business school. What you need is actionable advice designed for real life.

In your life, you may have come across a Natural Negotiator or two. They may not hold a business degree. They may never have taken a class in negotiation. Yet they seem to have an instinctual understanding of what to say and when and how to say it. Somehow, they seal the deal, with terms no one would ever have hoped for. They know something you don't learn in school.

We've all had certain dos and don'ts drilled into us from our first foray into the business world—adages like these:

- The person who says the first number loses.
- The negotiation doesn't start or stop until someone says no.
- You must make several concessions to get your bargaining partner to make a deal.
- The best negotiator can do it all—alone.

These truisms often leave people feeling like they can't succeed at negotiation. Their success may come at a steep cost, leaving the negotiation partner feeling bullied, swindled, or conned into a deal they didn't want. If the person you're negotiating with feels you are not at all flexible, you could sabotage your long-term relationship with them.

FIND OUT WHAT THEY REALLY WANT

Most of us walk into a negotiation with goals, ideas, and concessions we are willing to make. Be prepared not to get everything you want. Your opponent isn't Santa, and let's face it, even Santa never got you that pony. Take a tip from oil tycoon and successful businessman J. Paul Getty, who once said, "You must never try to make all the money in the deal. Let the other fellow make some money too, because if you have a reputation for always making all the money, you won't have many deals."[1] If you get everything you want, the other person will feel cheated, and this feeling will stay with them during all your future interactions. They will never quite feel whole and harbor ongoing resentment toward you.

We've broken down the road to negotiation mastery into three levels:

> **Level 1: Novice.** This is negotiation at the most basic level. It includes BATNA, win-wins, give and take. You are agreeing to terms based on what seems fair and unfair.
>
> **Level 2: Competent.** When you are at a level two, you have learned how to control your emotions. This includes self-regulation, being wise to your own tells, and knowing what will trigger positive or negative reactions from your opponent.
>
> **Level 3: Natural Negotiator.** At this level, you have mastered the skills of Levels 1 and 2, and you've become a natural. You consider your opponent's emotions and desires, you are clear and concise, you are free of worry and doubt, and you demonstrate your interest in helping the other party get what they want, to your mutual satisfaction.

Level 1: Novice Negotiator Example

Let's say you are negotiating a contract with a new vendor. You come to a stalemate on the terms of the agreement and price, but you get the sense they feel you are getting the better end of the deal, because they seem deflated and dejected with the number and terms.

Based on the previous conversation you had with this vendor, you can tell that their mood has changed, and they are not happy. They are agreeing, but their agreement seems insincere. We had a client once say, "Wow, you're really good at negotiation. I am not sure my manager will agree to this number. I know how they've worked with other vendors in your field, and I am not sure this is within reach. I will still try to do my best to get this number through our procurement office."

We knew, based on his slightly sarcastic tone, that this wasn't going to happen. It was clear they didn't feel we were trying hard enough to meet their needs. At this point, the negotiation was in serious jeopardy.

Most people don't like confrontation, but it isn't something you should shy away from. According to the CPP index, 49 percent of workplace conflict happens because of personality clashes and egos.[2] Not surprising, right? So if you are the source of conflict when a deal is being negotiated, the client will likely not want to take on more stress. They may pretend to agree and "promise to do their best," but they don't really want to make a deal. They are socially signaling to you that they are unhappy with the deal so far without coming right out and saying it. It is a test of how well you can or cannot work together, and this is where you can use some of the skills and convincing techniques you have learned in this book so far.

The Fix

Here's how you might frame a negotiation that has come to an impasse: "I am getting the sense you are unhappy with the terms. I want to make sure that we both get the deal we want and feel good about our relationship. There are some things I probably can't budge on—so I'm thinking it might be more productive if we pause here and take a look at this from a different perspective. How can we see this in a new way that will produce different thinking and allow us to get to the next stage?"

Level 2: Competent Negotiator Example

As a competent negotiator, you are in control of your own emotions. However, your negotiating partner is starting to make unreasonable demands. You can't come up with a solution to the current problem, so you stop the negotiation abruptly. This leaves the potential client uneasy (and not in a good way).

The Fix

If conflict is unavoidable and immediate, simply say something accommodating like: "You bring up some valid points," to make them feel acknowledged. If you're negotiating a contract, give yourself a cooling-off period. This gives your opponent what we refer to as "room to breathe."

More important, you need to get your emotions in check to keep your analytical brain from being hijacked by your fear of losing the deal. If taking a break is not possible, try shifting the conversation to topics you can both agree upon before returning to the contentious point.

Bill Coleman, a famed negotiator, used to advise people to "Count to 10. By then, the other person usually will start talking and may very well make a higher offer."[3] If you don't overdo it, your silence is a negotiation tactic in itself.

When Silence Is Not Golden

Silence can also show a lack of confidence. When I was in my mid-twenties, I was offered a vice president position at a big PR agency in New York City. The human resource manager who oversaw hiring brought up salary. On her own, she offered $10,000 more than initially put in the job ad. I was happy with this slight increase but wanted to press for more. I had nothing to lose because I already had a job. I was just looking for a better paying one. I paused and said nothing—using the silent technique.

At this point, the hiring manager started to lose her patience and said—"there is no more money for this position." I had enough experience to know it was a low offer, but I didn't speak up. I took the job but felt I was not being paid enough.

What I didn't know was that this hiring manager took this information and the feeling I left her with to my immediate supervisor. She resented my silent response and felt I had not demonstrated gratitude for her generosity. I know this because my supervisor brought it up. My boss said, "I know you don't feel you are being paid adequately." Now I initially brushed it off, but she was revealing something.

Shortly afterward, I found out a colleague, *who reported to me*, was being paid $15,000 more than me annually. The difference was she spoke up during her salary negotiation with the hiring manager, whereas I didn't.

Don't Overuse Silence as a Negotiation Tactic

For the sake of this being a learning example, let's look at my mistakes. I was using silence as a technique in the wrong way. I could have been more convincing if I had just given myself a moment to pause and counter the offer with a measured list of why I was more qualified. However, my mind was a blank. I was in fight, flight, or flee mode.

I should have mentioned that I had run national campaigns for brands with household names and successfully navigated crises for several high-profile clients, including two CEOs who were references for my employment. Additionally, I had won several industry accolades, including a "40 under 40" award for people in the PR industry. Yet I said nothing because I thought I was getting the upper hand by quietly holding my ground. Unfortunately, all I did was come across as defensive, and I didn't prove why I was worth more than the offer presented. Instead, in the end, I settled based on what the hiring manager thought I had done, not what I had accomplished in my career.

Here's what I should have done instead:

- I should have concentrated more on my goal and been more concise. I should have labeled the hiring manager's emotions. "I get the sense you feel I don't have the right experience for this position. Can we talk about why?"
- I should have taken away worry and doubt. Additionally, I should have validated the hiring manager's point of view regarding my compensation. This would have given her a way to increase the offer without losing face. "I understand why you may be hesitant to make me a higher offer. I also realize that this may seem like a higher salary than someone with my experience warrants, but I am not like the other candidates you may be talking to. Here's why."
- I should have showed I was looking to help her. I should have taken a moment to come back and provide a detailed list of my professional wins. This was such a huge lesson in my career that I later always had a printed, bound "brag book" with my résumé, writing samples, awards, and press clippings available for any interview I went on. Citing salary indexes from my industry would have also been smart. I could have demonstrated that this offer was not commensurate

with my experience. Instead, my lack of confidence created my silence.

Level 3: Natural Negotiator Example: How to Get Optimal Results Using the Flow State

When going into the Discovery Channel to pitch a reality show idea, we were negotiating the terms of the contract with producers for a client. This is something we get called in to do for big contracts where understanding and negotiating terms can get tricky. Chip and I had our team locked and ready to go with scripted roles and lines to say. The objections were all addressed with ease. The goal of this meeting we were leading was to decide on who the talent would be in the show and how much the two reality stars would be paid. At first, they offered the standard rate for reality shows per episode, which was roughly $2,500. It was a lowball offer. Next, they came up a little more in price to $3,000 per episode. Then they were trying to sell us on all the "advantages the business owners would get by having a free show" including "free airtime" on a major network. This was something we anticipated as well. Doing the show wasn't free. There was a lot of blood, sweat, and tears required for this type of production. Instead, we moved the conversation to what was different about what we had to offer:

- **Clear and concise.** We stressed how we started the trend, and no one other than the people being put forward could star in the show. This drove up the perceived value.
- **Take away worry and doubt.** We offered the producers an opportunity to keep the same rate per episode for one year if they came up in price to $4,500 per episode, even if the show took off.

- **Show we are looking to help them.** Hollywood is full of people looking for the "next big thing." They love the idea of potential opportunities. Natural Negotiators handle their own emotions with ease. They are armed with a host of ways *the negotiating partner will win.* Because a team member had done their due diligence, we knew one of the producers had had a few shows that had fallen just shy of being successful. There was also a rumor that some of the producer's higher-ups were starting to doubt his ability to find talent. That made us zero in on getting the producer excited about the "deal potential."

Chip used visioning techniques and predictive statements during the negotiation. He said, "Most people play it safe sometimes and also take risks when the moment is right. This seems like the type of calculated risk that makes careers." Naturally (pun intended), the producer took the risk, and we got the show produced.

Popularized by positive psychologists Mihaly Csikszentmihalyi and Jeanne Nakamura, "the flow state" describes the feeling of being fully immersed in your work so that the ideas come effortlessly, and the process feels almost organic. "There's this focus that, once it becomes intense, leads to a sense of ecstasy, a sense of clarity: you know exactly what you want to do from one moment to the other; you get immediate feedback," Csikszentmihalyi stated in a 2004 TED Talk.[4]

Remember, words leave clues and you are using all your convincing know-how. This is where you use what you have learned about someone through Forensic Listening to get them to a flow state. You are picking up on their subtle nuances, labeling emotions, looking at body positioning, and reacting in real time.

You are also analyzing your counterpart's Personality Baseline, Signature Personality Consistencies and Inconsistencies, and so on. Armed with all this knowledge, it will be up to you to think creatively about a solution that gets them in a flow state.

FLOAT ABOVE THE PROBLEMS TO ACHIEVE NEGOTIATION FLOW

One of our clients, let's call him Richard, was a chief negotiator for a government entity. He recounted being in the throes of a negotiation with a union leader. After lunch, Richard's counterpart became more and more aggravated. He quickly grew so unhelpful and combative that Richard suggested taking a break.

Looking back on what had transpired, Richard imagined himself floating above the conference room. He could see all the players in the negotiation, including himself. He noticed his counterpart furiously checking his phone, slamming it down in frustration every time he got a message. His attitude was deteriorating with every minute that went by. When Richard suggested a break for the day, he said, "Good idea," and quickly left the room.

The next day he came back, and his attitude was completely different—he was engaged, helpful, and creatively offering solutions. They concluded the negotiation in a way that was beneficial to both sides.

Richard couldn't miss the opportunity to find out why his counterpart's attitude had gone from disengaged to what could be described as a negotiation flow state. He approached his counterpart and asked. "I couldn't help but notice the massive change in your demeanor and openness to negotiate today as opposed to yesterday." The response explained a lot. "Yeah, I wanted to thank you for suggesting that we break early yesterday. My daughter had a soccer game, and I knew that the way things were going I was going to miss another one. So when you gave us the option to break, I was able to go to my daughter's soccer game." Richard's considerate question put his negotiation counterpart in a positive state of mind toward him and the negotiation process.

DISNEY CHAIRMAN ROBERT IGER— A NATURAL CONVINCER IN ACTION

Walt Disney Chairman Robert Iger is known as one of Hollywood's most talented negotiators. When he began talking to George Lucas about Disney acquiring the Star Wars franchise, Iger tread lightly. It took two years before the deal was done. In fact, you might say it was more of an ongoing conversation than a traditional negotiation. When asked about the deal, Iger would later point out that "There was a lot of trust there." The two years he spent getting to know Lucas were a prolonged exercise in convincing that paid off handsomely for Disney. According to an article in *Harvard Business Review*, "Disney promised to begin producing and releasing new films in the Star Wars franchise every two or three years. The acquisition even included a detailed script treatment for the next three *Star Wars* films."[5]

We would argue that the trust was built from what Iger sensed was Lucas's biggest fear—losing control of his creation once the deal was done. To address this, Iger didn't promise creative control over the franchise—which would be in Disney's hands. He knew talking about what Disney would do with the films wouldn't seal the deal. Instead, Iger did something brilliant from a negotiation standpoint. He invested in three spec scripts to show Lucas how *Star Wars* would live on.

This story is a perfect illustration of how a natural convincer operates:

- **Clear and concise.** Instead of just offering Lucas more money, Iger demonstrated that he understood the importance of Lucas's legacy.
- **Free of worry and doubt.** Iger allowed Lucas to handpick the producer of the next installment of *Star Wars*—a gesture of respect that ceded some control over the project to honor Lucas.
- **Sincere interest in helping others.** Iger understood that control over his legacy was what Lucas valued above all else. That was his currency.

What is your bargaining partner's emotional currency? Is it money, control, time, freedom from oversight? Make sure you get to the emotional reason for why someone is negotiating a deal, before offering concessions.

What we can take way from this multibillion-dollar deal is that a person is more likely to say yes if they feel seen and truly understood. If you take away what they value and want the most, you've lost.

In business, we are taught not to take anything personally during a negotiation. Experts have said, "Leave personalities out of it." We believe that this is bad advice. As people, we cannot simply cease to have emotions, even if we compartmentalize our feelings. Instead, what we recommend is analyzing the other person's relationship to money. Money is always tied to an emotion—either yours or the person you are negotiating with.

In HBR Ascend, Ramit Sethi said, "Our relationship to money is just as personal and valuable as any other relationship in our life."[6] And according to a PBS report, "Children can understand basic concepts about money as early as age 3, and by 7, their values around money are already set."[7] Therefore, figuring out someone's relationship to money and what it represents for them will contribute to the success of your negotiation.

Howard Baker said, "The most difficult thing in any negotiation is making sure that you strip it of emotion and deal with the facts." With all due respect to the senator, we contend that facts are always couched in emotion, especially when money is involved.

DON'T JUST CLOSE THE DEAL: CREATE A POSITIVE EMOTIONAL EXPERIENCE

Close the deal like a Natural Negotiator. The more you practice these principles, the more they will become second nature. Better yet, negotiating in this way will leave your counterpart with positive feelings about you and your business, opening the door for future fruitful negotiations down the road:

Step 1—Clear and concise. Let's say you are charged with closing a highly sought-after business to be a client. Your goal is clear.

Step 2—Free of worry and doubt. From extensive research and competitive intelligence, you know this particular business has been losing market share steadily over the past three quarters.

Step 3—Sincere interest in helping others. Your company may well be the best fit, offer the best service, and have reams of data on effectiveness and past successes.

Bonus Step for Natural Negotiators: Future-Casting

Let's say you did all the research into the specific areas of a prospect's business, and you know just which of your products or services will make a difference. You've prepared all the points to buttress your proposal. Your account rep presents all this information to the prospect, and yet they go with another firm. The other firm's package, price points, and presentation were all comparable. What happened?

Company B's account representative was connected to the client on an additional level. She wasn't just trying to close the deal. She was emotionally connecting with the customer. She was listening to their every word. She was dialed in to their needs, and she used one additional step we call Future-Casting. This is a process in which you use case studies and stories that demonstrate experience and expertise. Your rival convinced the prospect that this deal was something her company had done repeatedly, with predictable levels of success.

Like you, she did her homework, and she knew that the prospect's company had suffered a downturn. It's tempting in such cases to play dumb and ignore the elephant in the room, but that's not what your rival did. She made it a point to ask probing, open-ended questions and had candid conversations about the situation with the prospect, even asking how this was affecting him and senior leadership. She demonstrated empathy with statements like, "This must be making everyone anxious about the future," and "People must be worried about their positions," and "There must be a lot of pressure on you to find solutions."

During her presentation, she was able to connect the solutions her company was offering as a means of helping the prospect's company rebound. She forged a powerful connection through empathy, Forensic Listening, and a positive vision of the prospect company's future.

Businesspeople can become too fixated on getting the sale, like it's the only thing that matters. Closing the deal becomes a crippling mental block that gets in the way of forging a long-term relationship. When we focus on outcomes and not process, we lose more deals than we win.

When you feel like the deal is slipping away, your stress level begins to rise. You may appear desperate. Your prospect can sense it, which makes it stressful to deal with you. By paying attention to the process rather than obsessing over the potential result, you're building a foundation for future deals.

You have control over yourself, the message you present, the quality of the questions you ask, and the amount of preparation you and your team do before a meeting. As stated previously, you do not have control over what your prospect or negotiation counterpart will do. But you can control the quality and strength of the connection you develop.

KEY TAKEAWAYS

- A Natural Negotiator conducts negotiations with concentration and clarity, freedom from worry and doubt, and a passion for helping others achieve their goals.
- Try to identify your bargaining partner's emotional currency. Is it money, control, time, freedom from oversight? Make sure you get to the emotional reason for why someone is negotiating a deal before offering concessions.
- A person is more likely to say yes if they feel seen and truly understood. If you take away what they value and want the most, you've lost.
- We are taught not to take anything personally during a negotiation. Experts have said "leave personalities out of it." We believe that this is bad advice. As people we cannot simply cease to have emotions, even if we compartmentalize our feelings. Instead, what we recommend is analyzing the other person's relationship to money. Money is always tied to an emotion—either yours or the person with whom you are negotiating.

CHAPTER 14

THE ROLE FEAR PLAYS IN HIGH-STAKES SITUATIONS

Judging people by the worst moment of their life is absurd. In fact, the smallest percentage of your life is when you are at your worst. We don't approach any other thing in life that way. For instance, we don't use the smallest percentage of anything to determine a possible outcome. That would be like not doing something because it is 99.9 percent safe and basing that decision on the infinitesimal time it might be unsafe. Yet the age-old adage persists—the notion that character can be determined by how you manage in a crisis. This idea is so ingrained in our society that people are afraid to prepare for worst-case scenarios for fear of what it might reveal about them.

If you had asked me on September 10, 2001, how I would react to witnessing the worst terrorist act to ever occur on American soil, I would have assumed I'd be freaking out with everybody else. Instead, my journalistic training kicked in. I walked into a store and bought a cheap camera. When I came out, I started taking photographs.

I learned something about myself that day: I have a built-in crisis mode. In everyday life, I am as emotional as the next Italian American Jersey girl. In a crisis, my inner Brit takes over: I keep calm and carry on. The truth is, none of us know how we will react in a crisis, whether it's a natural disaster, a serious car accident, a life-or-death situation involving a loved one, or a PR debacle that threatens your company, your brand, and your livelihood.

As people who help leaders through high-stakes business situations, we've seen our share of precarious, highly sensitive situations. What we have found is that the best leaders have had these types of experience before and understand that fear is part of the equation. How you deal with the fear determines how good or bad the outcome will be.

MASTERING FEAR

How does your mastery of fear affect your decision-making? What kinds of mistakes might you make? Here are a few examples drawn from our experience:

- **Withdrawal.** The board president who froze every time he had to assert himself and make a critical decision, a response our client referred to as "turtling."
- **Panic.** The CEO who made too many decisions too fast, like a drowning person holding on to whatever she can

grab to keep from sinking. In a high-stakes business situation, you must move quickly, not frantically.

- **Analysis paralysis.** The C-suite exec who knew he must respond and desperately wanted to, but by the time he got through all the pros and cons of a move, it was too late.
- **Savior syndrome.** The hero-wannabe who insisted on handling everything herself and ended up taking on way more than she could realistically accomplish. Letting your ego take over is one way to miss ancillary threats and overlook important details.

What's important to understand is that all these reactions to stress are perfectly normal. You need to know yourself and your patterns of behavior so you don't keep making the same mistakes.

For Chip and me, the ideal type of leader to work with was the scarily calm CEO. They understood the stakes and responded with discipline and gravitas. The ability to delegate is critical in leadership, provided the leader picks the right core team. They consulted a limited number of people with particular areas of expertise, kept their staff informed, followed our advice, and responded within hours.

ANCIENT BRAIN, MODERN WORLD

The human brain evolved over one million years ago and is not set up to assess modern-day risk. As advanced primates, we are wired to scan our environment to determine whether someone is a friend or enemy. We anticipate potential danger.

We interviewed American cryptographer, computer security professional, privacy specialist, and writer Bruce Schneier for this book. He had a lot to say about the primitive brain, best summarized in an article he wrote for *Wired*:[1]

> Assessing and reacting to risk is one of the most important things a living creature must deal with, and there's a very primitive part of the brain that has that job. It's the amygdala, and it sits right above the brainstem, in what's called the medial temporal lobe. The amygdala is responsible for processing base emotions that come from sensory inputs, like anger, avoidance, defensiveness, and fear. (More on this in Chapter 9.)

The *Wired* article explains that when early primates experienced intense danger, such as being attacked by a saber-toothed tiger, their brains developed a protective lifelong fear. As Schneier sees it, "Your brain is being trained to think, 'If this happened once, it could happen again. If it does, I will be ready.'" Essentially, how you respond to fear is a habit. Like most habits, it can be changed with the right training and experience.

THE CAMERA AND THE DOUBLE AGENT

Army Ranger. CIA case officer. Trainer of hundreds of CIA recruits. Respected intelligence officer. Harold Nicholson was everything a CIA case agent should be, until he started to raise suspicions within the FBI.

As a new special agent in the FBI, Chip was assigned to the espionage squad in the Washington, DC, field office. "We were working a joint case with the CIA, and we had identified a penetration into the organization," he recalled. "One of the senior case officers was a double agent working for the Russian Intelligence Service, providing highly classified information on our intelligence programs. This prompted a full-blown espionage investigation because he was identified as an intelligence agent being controlled by a hostile foreign power."

One of Chip's responsibilities was to monitor his subject's actions via a hidden camera the FBI had installed in Nicholson's office. Chip was in the monitoring room the day before the spy was supposed to travel to Switzerland to deliver classified documents to his Russian handlers. The FBI planned to arrest Harold Nicholson once he boarded the plane to travel to Switzerland.

Chip remembers everything looking perfectly normal that day—at first. Nicholson was working in his office—just like all the other days Chip's team had surveilled him. He was typing on his computer, drinking coffee, and filing documents. Then he started pulling on wires on his desk, lifting up his desk phone, and looking underneath it. He was clearly looking for something.

Chip got on the phone to alert people on the squad to what was happening. Was the suspect onto them? The FBI surveillance room, which was about the size of a broom closet, began to fill up with members of the espionage squad.

Thirty minutes later, Nicholson stopped what he was doing again and got down on his hands and knees under his desk, likely continuing to search for evidence of surveillance equipment. As the tension mounted in the surveillance room, Nicholson got back in his chair and resumed his regular routine. Approximately 15 minutes went by, and he stopped, pushed away from his desk, and looked straight up at the drop ceiling. Nicholson climbed up on his chair. "Although I could only see from his belt level down," Chip remembers, "it was obvious that he was pushing up tiles looking for a camera. We thought the operation might be compromised."

At this point, the room was full of senior officials from the FBI Washington field office as well as the people who had installed the surveillance camera. Everyone was holding their breath waiting for static to appear on the screen—the moment he would discover the camera and flee. Chip recalls:

> We put out an alert to the physical surveillance team to be extremely vigilant. Surveillance was instructed to keep him in sight at all times. We planned to arrest him if he deviated even slightly from his normal routine. The good news was he stuck to his regular route and went home. We had a team of special agents close to his house to watch his movements. The next day, Nicholson showed up at the airport. We had agents in the bookstore, coffee shop—even the person manning the airport gate was on Team America. Airport security cameras were also being monitored.

Nicholson was one of the last people to board his plane. Once he took his seat, two FBI agents boarded the plane, identified themselves, and asked him to come with them. At first, Nicholson started to tense up like he might resist arrest, but it was clear resistance was futile. He was caught and he knew there was no way out. He was escorted to a car, transported to a building at the airport, and informed he was under arrest for espionage. At that time, he refused to cooperate or provide any information. However, over the course of preparing for his trial, it became apparent to Nicholson's attorney that the government's case was airtight, and Nicholson would be facing the death penalty. He changed his mind and agreed to cooperate fully with the FBI.

Cooperation meant revealing how Russia directed their embedded operatives. Was Nicholson being paid? How did the Russians communicate with him? In truth, the FBI mostly wanted Nicholson to confirm what they already knew, but the interviews yielded a detail that still surprises Chip, many years later:

> Over the course of multiple interview sessions, we asked Nicholson if he ever searched his office for signs of surveillance equipment. He acted insulted and responded with an emphatic "No." He said he had searched and there was nothing there to find. We were shocked.
>
> A highly trained, seasoned CIA case officer who knew everything about these cameras had missed the one hidden in the drop ceiling in his office. There was no way Nicholson should have missed that camera, even though it was installed by the very best in the FBI. He would have been very aware of the techniques, capabilities, equipment, and requirements for surveillance camera installation. He knew what to look for and still missed it. Why? We believe, he was so consumed with his deal with the Russians, his brain simply wouldn't let him see the camera. Fear made the camera invisible.

Harold James Nicholson was the second highest-ranking CIA employee to be caught spying and plead guilty to the espionage violation. He also agreed to tell federal investigators what secrets he gave away and to turn over all his property to the government. Nicholson is currently serving life in prison.

If we let our primitive brain override our decision-making, we miss critical things. When this type of stress takes over, you are not at your best. You'll miss important details and overlook possible solutions and would likely benefit from an outside perspective. Nicholson was so invested in his lies that he did not want to face the truth. The fact is, no one wants to believe in the truth if the truth does not make them an expert anymore. Seeing the camera would have invalidated Nicholson's CIA expertise, identity, and life as a double agent.

This is why it is so hard to accept that we should prepare for a reputational or business crisis. We inaccurately assume that saying we need a plan because we may not be totally equipped to handle an issue casts aspersion on our character and our level of expertise. Leaders feel this may make them less influential and therefore less effective. However, when a leader can lean into fear, they become more convincing to those around them.

USING AND SPOTTING FEAR-BASED CONVINCING TACTICS IN BUSINESS

In a business crisis, executives fear for their reputation and livelihood. They are gravely concerned about how members of the media and the public are judging their every decision.

So what separates a leader who successfully rebounds from and even thrives after a huge crisis from one who struggles to recover? The answer is the ability to handle and harness fear. Like many if not most clichés, the saying about the hidden opportunity at the heart of every crisis is true. It's often undetected, slipping in through the back door while everyone is transfixed by unfolding events. Identifying and seizing that opportunity can create huge momentum for your business after a crisis. It can determine whether you hit the ground running or suffer a serious setback.

So how do you handle fear? First, you need to understand your physical, mental, and emotional reactions when you're afraid. Let's say you've just heard some bad news. It can be a major issue (like a global crisis) or a minor issue (like a project deadline, impatient boss, or angry client). Your body reacts, either way. Your adrenal gland starts pumping out the stress hormones adrenaline and cortisol. Your heart rate and blood pressure shoot up. Your nervous system inhibits your nonessential body functions so you can focus your energy on crisis control.

It's a useful response when you're face-to-face with a grizzly bear and need to go into fight-or-flight mode. But that fear response doesn't do you a bit of good if you're trying to finish a project with your boss breathing down your neck. Your ability to reason is often the first victim of that system downgrade. Another casualty of the fear response is your ability to see and hear with discernment. This explains why workplace stress can cause brain freeze and dry mouth just when you need to be thinking fast and speaking coherently.

Actual Versus Assumed Dangers

The problem is the way our brains are wired. For all its marvels, the mind does a terrible job of discerning between actual and assumed dangers. It assigns the same emotional response to social distress as it does to survival situations. The more intense the social distress, the more likely our brain identifies it as a physical threat.

HOW A LEADER MASTERS FEAR

Insight is an essential aspect of leadership—insight into situations, people, and yourself. It's essential that you know your fear style to keep it from dragging you down. When a crisis hits, literally take a breather. Resist the impulse to freak out, get on the phone, or call an immediate meeting at which hand-wringing will be the number one agenda item. Instead, take a tip from an NPR interview "Just Breathe: Body Has a Built-in Stress Reliever."[2]

Go into your office, close the door, close your eyes, and breathe. Relax, slow down, calm yourself. Your body may be reacting to a grizzly bear, but your mind knows there's no bear in the room.

Once you feel grounded and calm, it's time to take the team out of survival mode. Chip has spent a great deal of time doing this as an FBI special agent and hostage negotiator. I too have done this countless times throughout my career as crisis communication expert, with clients ranging from President Joe Biden to CEOs, CMOs, and CCOs from a broad swath of industries.

Getting Your Team to Chill

Keep an open door and an open mind. This is a time when your team needs to hear from you.

- **Don't procrastinate.** It's human nature to want to wait for a bad situation to magically blow over. But curiosity is human nature too. As soon as people find out your company is experiencing "a situation," they will want to know more. Silence leads to mistrust, suspicion, and speculation. Speculation engenders rumors and rumors spread quickly.

- **Address the fear.** If you run away from fear or fail to address it, it will still be blaring in the back of everyone's minds, totally drowning out anything you have to say. Instead, acknowledge the fear, label it as a normal response and ease your team out of it by reframing it as an opportunity. Putting people's fear front and center takes the sting out of it and creates an opportunity for community, dialogue, suggestions, and solutions.
- **Don't gamble with the truth.** While addressing internal organizational fear, you must address external perceptions, both accurate and inaccurate. If you don't, folks will fill in the blanks by speculating. Of course, some things may have to remain confidential, but share as much of the truth as you can.
- **Can the rationalizations.** Your team deserves better. What they want from you in a time of crisis is authenticity. People can see right through platitudes like these:
    - "The other person/group/company is at fault. Not us."
    - "Yeah, some people are mad about this [fill in the blank], but our company will survive."
    - "People are really making a big deal out of one small mistake. Let's just wait for it to blow over."
    - "We've experienced setbacks in the past and will continue to do so. There's no need to overreact."
    - "We can survive a few bad headlines/reviews/comments/missteps—people know what we stand for as a company."
    - "Let's see where we are tonight/tomorrow/next week and reassess."

FROM FEAR TO THE FUTURE

That's right, the number one most powerful emotion we can trigger to gain back respect is none other than fear. The trick lies in taking the fear that people are experiencing and bridging it to future expectations. By talking about it, addressing the problem, and facing what happened head on, you strengthen your position as a leader. If this is the worst thing that's happened under your leadership, and you don't move people from fear to the future fast enough, people will lose hope.

Here are three statements you can implement to create curiosity and faith in your vision:

> **Option 1.** "Fear is our brains letting us know we are entering a new phase of possibility. Let's use this crisis to move the organization forward. I'm curious what you think we should do as we move into the future. Any ideas?"
>
> **Option 2.** "They say every crisis is an opportunity. Where do you think this can help us improve the organization and strengthen it? I have some ideas to share, but I wanted to hear your perspective." (Then use Forensic Listening techniques recommended in Chapter 2.)
>
> **Option 3.** "How do you think our leaders might benefit from us taking a powerful move forward? What opportunities exist for us now that weren't there before? Here's three ways I think we can benefit . . ."

Naturally, you don't need to say it exactly like this (you'll want to translate it into your own tone and style), but the message is clear.

Bad things come to those who wait.

Procrastination is the biggest, earliest, and often costliest mistake you can make in a crisis. You have a very short window in which to plan your defense strategy. Don't waste it. Too many leaders waste precious time convincing themselves and others around them that they don't need to react to a situation that threatens their company.

Most leaders who opt to wait out a few bad headlines don't realize they could be slowly losing trust. This leads to speculation, and people tend to assume the worst. Let's face it, negative speculation is way more entertaining than giving you the benefit of the doubt. As everyone well knows, people like stories. If you don't find a way to tell yours, your audience will make one up.

In the late 1950s, the psychiatrist Klaus Conrad coined the term "apophenia" to describe our tendency to perceive connections between unrelated things. Whether it's a face emerging from the wallpaper or a conspiracy theory cobbled together from random facts, the brain wants to see patterns. Your audience will use reference points from current events to turn your crisis into a story. You are especially vulnerable if the situation you're facing reflects something that's happening in the culture—for example—a sexual harassment issue in the Me-too era.

In our social-media-fueled age of rumors and conspiracy theories, controlling the message is more important than ever before. It doesn't help that the culture has ADHD. Folks just want the top line—forget about nuance and details. You're getting judged in the court of public opinion, and you must be your own defense attorney.

Some leaders respond to the public's hunger for information by putting out a single generic holding statement—something vague like, "We will get back to you when we have more information." This is the equivalent of a telephone hold message—all they are doing is annoying people. They may release a tepid follow-up or not even bother, in the hopes that people will have moved on to the next story. That's a major error. All they're doing is calling attention to the issue—a second opportunity for the public to fill in the blanks. Not only does the first statement need to be specific, but it also must be followed up by regular updates to fill the silence so people don't have the time to speculate.

KEY TAKEAWAYS

- Fear has an adverse effect on decision-making. Common responses are withdrawal, panic, analysis paralysis, and savior syndrome.
- Procrastination is the biggest, earliest, and often costliest mistake you can make in a crisis. You have a very short window in which to plan your defense strategy. Too many leaders waste precious time convincing themselves and others around them that they don't need to react to a situation that threatens their company.
- At the heart of every crisis is an opportunity. While it's often undetected because most people are transfixed by unfolding events, identifying and seizing that opportunity can create huge momentum for your business after a crisis.

- In leading a team in a fear-inducing crisis, the trick lies in taking the fear that people are experiencing and bridging it to future expectations. By talking about it, addressing the problem, and identifying a path forward, you strengthen your position as a leader.

CHAPTER 15

CONVINCE AS ONLY YOU CAN: YOUR PERSONAL CONVINCING STYLE

"It's complicated," said John F. Kennedy, Jr., shifting a bit in his seat as he pondered how to answer his interviewer, CNN's Larry King. The questions Larry was asking were personal and direct. What is it like being the son of a president and cultural icon? How does it feel to be junior to a legendary father? John answered honestly. "It makes for a rich and complicated life, and it's a puzzle I have to figure out."[1]

John's response was disarming but slightly disingenuous. The truth is, John F. Kennedy, Jr., was a master at managing people's perceptions and expectations. He knew he needed to address and debunk the snap judgments they might have made and move them past their preconceptions about him. He had to make them see beyond:

- The sad little boy saluting at his father's funeral
- The jet-setting son of a stylish and sophisticated former First Lady, Jacqueline Kennedy Onassis
- The shirtless heartthrob who failed the New York Bar Exam three times before finally passing
- The silver spoon baby who seemingly had everything handed to him by his wealthy, famous parents

John was acutely aware that any of these four preconceptions could impact his interactions, making effective communication very complicated indeed. Knowing how people see you is challenging for all of us, but it's a critical convincing skill. If you anticipate people's preconceptions about you and your objectives, you can strategize to maximize your influence.

As you read this chapter, you will learn how to establish your story and professional style to boost your persuasive powers.

HOW I MET JOHN F. KENNEDY, JR.

I was in my early twenties and needed an internship to complete my degree from Rutgers University. I was a double major in journalism and political science and assistant editor at the school newspaper *The Targum*. *George* magazine was my dream internship. John Kennedy, Jr., had launched a cultural phenomenon, mixing pop culture, celebrity, and politics in a revolutionary way. Who better than John, who had spent his entire life in the public eye, to explore those connections?

I reached out to a fellow Rutgers graduate, Richard Blow, the editor in chief at *George* magazine and got him to agree to an interview for a profile in the school's newspaper. (Yes, I was convincing even then!) After we sat and talked for an hour, I summoned all the moxie of a first-generation college graduate and said, "Hey, now that I know so much about your magazine . . . are you looking for interns?" Blow offered me the position on the spot.

By the time I arrived at the spectacular skyscraper at 1633 Broadway on my first day, my mother had told anyone who would listen that I had landed an internship at *George* magazine, with the real, live, honest to goodness John F. Kennedy, Jr. Feeling both nervous and excited, I took the elevator to *George* magazine's forty-first floor offices, where I was greeted by one of John's assistants. She gave me a very specific set of rules for interacting with John—I was told exactly how to treat him, what to call him, and how to approach him.

John, and by extension, his assistant, understood that like everyone else, I was joining *George* with my own set of preconceived notions about its founder. While John's magazine was a cultural phenomenon, he was still struggling to build his own influence as an individual apart from his famous parents. The assistant was shifting my perceptions of John to maximize his influence and position at the magazine. Above all, she emphasized to never, ever call him John-John. It was just John, and he was to be treated like everyone else in the office. "If you can't do that," she warned, "you won't survive your first week."

I was witnessing a convincing strategy being successfully deployed by one of the most acutely self-aware public figures of the nineties. It is a strategy I have occasionally deployed myself, to this day. Here's how John took control of his own narrative to make people treat him the way he wanted to be treated:

- He addressed people's perceptions and misperceptions about him up front because he didn't want his public persona to get in the way of a free exchange of ideas.
- Craving genuine, unfettered bullpen interactions, he created a culture at *George* magazine where deferential sycophants would not be rewarded. Instead, he openly praised those who pushed back fearlessly and treated him like a fellow journalist and regular leader.
- He set boundaries. Having his assistant brief me before I met him was a boundary in itself. Professional boundaries must be clearly stated, reasons must be given—but by setting them—you are telling others you are a person worth listening to. You don't need an administrative assistant to do it.

John F. Kennedy, Jr., was smart, warm, engaging, approachable and above all else, acutely aware of how people saw him. He would kid around with the entire staff, even lowly interns like me. He knew my name and made me feel like a big deal. I'll never forget how he treated me and everyone else around him. This lasting impression remains powerful as ever in the years since John's untimely death in 1999.

BUILDING THE BASELINE PERSONALITY

John's strategic approach is something we can all put into practice. Of course, most of us don't have to worry about fame and an illustrious backstory coloring other people's perceptions. We likely lack the clout and the trusted inner circle to help us shape our image. Nonetheless, based on previous personal experience, we should all have some sense of how people perceive us.

Every one of us has had the experience of walking into a situation weighed down by the prejudgments of others. It could be due to the power dynamics inherent in the interaction and whether you are seen as having the upper hand. It could be as basic as how you look or dress or the people you associate with. Perhaps it's your tone of voice, your opening statement, or the fact that you remind them of their ex (good luck with that one).

As the saying goes, you never get a second chance to make a first impression. The first time you meet someone, both of you are building a foundation for your future relationship. You're forging an understanding of each other's baseline personalities, an understanding that will deepen over future interactions. In that initial meeting, you have three things to accomplish:

1. **The meeting agenda.** Whether it's an interview, a presentation, a briefing—this is the actual business reason you are meeting this person.
2. **Establishing your baseline personality.** You may not have an assistant to lay the groundwork for you the way John F. Kennedy, Jr., did, but you are entirely in control of the impression you make.
3. **Reading the other person's baseline personality.** Think of this as a sketch that you can fill in and correct over time.

Piercing Through Preconceived Notions

We've all gotten into situations where false assumptions are being made about us, just as we make them about others. You can certainly get better at reading others, and this book will help you do that. But what about how others perceive you? When it comes to the impression you make, either you write the script, or they will do it for you.

To understand how people perceive you, you must be mindful of your own patterns and behaviors. Therefore, you must be keenly aware of the intent of your interactions. Be clear about what you hope to give and get out of every interaction you have.

Being an accurate reader of how you come across means taking a step back to ask: "Do other people know I think this way?" One of the greatest challenges in understanding how you are perceived by others is knowing exactly how people will read you. It is a form of mental modeling, as defined in an article in *Fast Company*, "A mental model is an explanation of the thought process a person uses when moving through the world. . . . Everyone's mental models are different because they're founded in different life experiences. By trying to understand other people's mental models, you are attempting to make sense of why they behave the way they do."[2]

To do this, people routinely assess each other's mindsets (beliefs, knowledge, ignorance) in social interactions. We do what psychologist Endel Tulving called "mental time traveling" to predict what others might say over the course of a conversation.

To help you better predict how you come across, we've developed a How People Perceive You Scorecard. Our scorecard will give you a sense of how others might analyze you in four different scenarios. This will enable you to accurately predict whether your interaction will be positive or negative.

Once you have a good list, give yourself a plus sign (+) for a positive way people react to you. Or a negative sign (–) if people don't react well to what you do. Last, write an equal (=) sign to represent a neutral reaction. The marks you give to each interaction will depend on your goals.

HOW PEOPLE PERCEIVE YOU SCORECARD, SITUATION 1

In this interaction, you are asking someone whom you have no real managerial authority over to complete a task that is critical to your success. Although you've interacted with them several times in the past, you still have difficulty knowing whether they will comply with your request. Here's how to read how this person reads you.

How do they greet you before you talk about the project details?
Positive, Negative, or Neutral

Do they ask you questions about your request?
Positive, Negative, or Neutral

Do you ask them questions about their role in the project?
Positive, Negative, or Neutral

Do they follow up regarding your answers and show an interest in achieving the desired goal?
Positive, Negative, or Neutral

Are their questions related to the project directed toward your needs as opposed to their own?
Positive, Negative, or Neutral

Are they actively showing an interest in getting the project done?
Positive, Negative, or Neutral

Do they treat you differently than they did before you made the request?
Positive, Negative, or Neutral

When they talk about the project with others, do they seem enthusiastic?
Positive, Negative, or Neutral

As stated in Situation 1, if you are trying to get promoted into a leadership role and people who are at the same level as you often refuse to do what you ask, even if it is a small request, you are unlikely to be chosen for that position. While seemingly innocuous, those behaviors would be a negative on your scorecard.

However, if people react with enthusiasm to your request and follow-through, that would be a positive. Likewise, if people do the task for everyone the same way they do it for you, that may be considered neutral, which would warrant an equal sign on your scorecard.

HOW PEOPLE PERCEIVE YOU SCORECARD, SITUATION 2

In this interaction, you are the supervisor, and you need to get your employees to get a new sales target. You know there is some resistance from your team regarding how you should go about achieving this goal. The last sales target was not met, *due to unforeseen circumstances*, and you believe people's confidence in your leadership is waning. How do you get a sense of what the group is thinking and address preconceived perceptions and misperceptions?

When you announce a new sales target, what is people's initial reaction to the goal?
Positive, Negative, or Neutral

Are there supporters in your group who agree with the direction of the target?
Positive, Negative, or Neutral

When people talk about the impact of reaching the goal, do they demonstrate enthusiasm?
Positive, Negative, or Neutral

Do you have one person on your team who questions your direction in group meetings?
Positive, Negative, or Neutral

Is there a lot of talk about the previous project that failed?
Positive, Negative, or Neutral

Do people on your team seem concerned about how others in the company will view achieving or not achieving the goal?
Positive, Negative, or Neutral

How do people on your team frame challenges?
Positive, Negative, or Neutral

Do they believe the sales target is attainable?
Positive, Negative, or Neutral

How people perceive you in various interactions will ultimately enable you to consistently predict what others will expect of you and determine whether you can get what you want from future interactions.

Once you have a good list of interactions, think about whether these behaviors are helping you be perceived the way you want to be. Are you effectively modeling the behaviors you want to see more of from others? Do these interactions cast a vote for or against your desired credibility? Observe your interactions without judgment, and focus on recognizing how people you view and what triggers these viewpoints.

How do people read you in your emails and texts? Think about how you leave people feeling. Is it positive or negative? All of these things have short-term and long-term effects on how you are perceived.

HOW PEOPLE PERCEIVE YOU SCORECARD, SITUATION 3

In this interaction, you are considering how you come across on email. You are asking colleagues to participate in a professional development opportunity. This is not mandatory training. However, the amount of participation will demonstrate your ability to lead. How do you come across to your coworkers on this type of an email?

Do you start your emails with a bonding rapport technique like: Hope you are all well?
Yes, No, or Neutral

Do you immediately explain why you are sending the email?
Yes, No, or Neutral

Are there examples of people your email audience can relate to who benefited from the training?
Yes, No, or Neutral

Do you encourage the reader to envision an end goal?
Yes, No, or Neutral

Is there a reminder that it is the reader's choice to take action or not?
Yes, No, or Neutral

Did you create an actionable subject line with a deadline?
Yes, No, or Neutral

Is it clear what the next action people need to take?
Yes, No, or Neutral

One of the most popular video platforms, Zoom is used by 350 million people daily. Video conference calls are a big part of the corporate work experience. Making sure you show up the right way is critical for success.

HOW PEOPLE PERCEIVE YOU SCORECARD, SITUATION 4

In this interaction, you are on a video call.

Do you show up early, on time, or late?
Positive, Negative, or Neutral

Are you mindful of what your background says about you?
Positive, Negative, or Neutral

Are you multitasking while on the Zoom call, that is, reading emails and sending messages?
Positive, Negative, or Neutral

What is the other person's level of eye contact with you?
Positive, Negative, or Neutral

Are you looking at a phone?
Positive, Negative, or Neutral

Do you end the call and make it clear what the next steps are?
Positive, Negative, or Neutral

Does the call end on time or late?
Positive, Negative, or Neutral

TABLE 15.1 Strategic Move Versus Hoping for the Best

Strategic Move	Versus	Hoping for the Best
You have one clear goal about how you want others to perceive you. For example, "Before we leave, we need to address this one thing."		You don't plan what to say or the outcomes of the meetings.
You make it clear what you stand for and use examples with built-in authority to prove your point. For example, "I read a quote about Jeff Bezos, and I like how he approaches business growth."		No one knows what you stand for or who influences your decisions or approach.
You are aware of how others viewed you emotionally because you track it and readdress how everyone is feeling.		You take notes about what happened and what to do next.
You know how you have come across. For example, you want others to see you as "thoughtful," so you prop up coworkers' contributions.		You don't have intention about what you highlight, and the lack of consistency makes it difficult for people to predict your behavior.

KEY TAKEAWAYS

- We've all gotten into situations where false assumptions are being made about us, just as we make them about others. When it comes to the impression you make, either you write the script, or they will do it for you.
- To help you better predict how you come across, we've developed a How People Perceive You Scorecard. Our scorecard will give you a sense of how others might analyze you in four different scenarios. This will enable you to accurately predict whether your interaction will be positive or negative.

CHAPTER 16

THE FOUR ESSENTIAL ELEMENTS OF EFFECTIVE CONVINCING

You don't have to be a genius to get people to do what you want, you just have to be convincing. This prescriptive chapter will provide some simple strategies to help you gain more clarity and confidence in business and in life.

We will focus on the importance of delivering the right message at the right time. That means factoring in the four essential elements of effective convincing: timing, believability, likability, and repeatability.

TIMING

Creating an effective convincing strategy requires a sophisticated approach to timing—what you say matters a lot, but when you say it can sabotage you. For example, if you are thinking about asking for a raise, figuring out the best time to ask is a big part of whether you will be successful.

Here's some advice from Captain Obvious: If you know the person you are convincing has a lot on their mind, back off. You don't ask for a raise when your boss's child is in the hospital, or the company is having layoffs, or there's a new CEO and layoffs are rumored. If your boss leaves work at 5:00 sharp to go to the gym, asking for that raise at 4:55 isn't going to work for you. On the other hand, let's say that same boss just got promoted, partly for winning a new account with more than a little help from you. This would be the perfect time to ask for your raise or promotion. The boss is happy, testing their new power, and maybe even convinced of your value and grateful for your help. Now's the time to get in there and ask for that raise!

Timing is just as important when trying to convince a broader audience. Convincing is marketing's raison d'être. If you're raising awareness, you're trying to convince consumers to consider your brand. If you're selling a specific product or service, you're attempting to persuade people to buy it. As PR experts, we work with you to understand current trends, peaks in interest, and the buzz about you and your industry or profession. Once you understand when others (media and customers) are thinking about someone with your expertise, you can predict the best time to weigh in on related news and events.

Let's say you are a fitness expert. You probably think late December to early January is the ideal time to advertise. People are overeating, drinking too much, and too busy to work out.

Their clothes are getting tight. Then comes New Year's Eve and all those enthusiastic New Year's resolutions. So this is when you want to make your pitch, right? Sure, if you want your communication to be yet another ripple in a sea of sameness. But what if you were to wait until January 17, the day when, according to *Psychology Today*, the most people give up on their resolution?[1] Buck the trend by sharing this interesting factoid when your competition has gone quiet, and guilt people back into working out.

Timing is one of the most basic elements to consider when convincing, but this is where many fall short. When does your audience expect to hear from you? When do they *want* to hear from you? What might trigger a response in industry that even internal and external stakeholders would recognize as an opportunity for you or your company to be a part of the conversation?

BELIEVABILITY

The basics of good storytelling haven't changed since early humans first gathered around a fire to hear a recap of the day's hunt. You need an intriguing beginning, or "hook" (the thing everyone can agree on), a middle that will keep people reading (Convincing Cliffhanger), and a satisfying ending. Your convincing strategy and approach should feel honest and true and follow a solid storytelling structure. Most important, your story must be believable.

Remember the Eads Bridge story from Chapter 4? Carnegie promised that his bridge was safe. When folks remained skeptical, he came up with a hook: having an elephant cross the bridge in front of 300,000 onlookers, at a packed Independence Day parade. No matter that this stunt did nothing to prove the bridge's long-term safety—people wanted to believe the bridge was safe and the elephant convinced them.

It's essential that what you are saying be not just believable, but also truthful. Lies have a way of backfiring and can seriously damage your reputation. A historic example of this is the story of Thomas Edison and Tesla. Dubbed the "Wizard of Menlo Park," Edison was an incredible prolific inventor, with 1,093 US patents to his name. Over the course of his career, Edison averaged a patent a week. Yet he almost lost everything trying to convince the public alternating current (AC) was dangerous.

Serbian physicist Nikola Tesla was just a poor inventor when he first went to see Edison to discuss his idea of using AC to generate electricity. Tesla naively thought he was going to meet a fellow genius who shared his passion for invention. Instead, he encountered a fierce competitor who would not easily give up the spotlight.

Tesla was not prepared to deal with Edison, the businessman. Edison understood money and cared about turning a profit. Indeed, many of Edison's patents were taken out proactively, when the invention was barely a blip in the great man's brain, years before he would get around to building a prototype. Edison was also adept at convincing and PR, long before PR was a mainstream business practice. Tesla had no such financial or marketing sophistication. He was a true science geek and didn't concern himself with how people perceived him. This inability to burnish his own image to help promote his ideas would be an issue for Tesla his whole life.

Edison was a bona fide celebrity, arguably the most famous scientist of his time. He had already built several power plants in the United States and Europe, using direct current (DC) technology. He needed to keep his investors happy. Tesla's idea of using AC could potentially supplant DC technology and send Edison back to square one.

The major advantage AC has over DC is that AC voltages are easily transformed to higher or lower voltage levels. High voltages are more efficient for sending electricity great distances, giving AC electricity a clear advantage over DC. Using Edison's DC method, one plant could generate maybe 10 square blocks of electricity, whereas Tesla's idea had the potential to light up entire cities.

According to Tesla, Edison promised him $50,000 to do some challenging repairs on one of his plants. When Tesla tried to collect, Edison claimed he had been kidding about the $50,000 and refused to pay. Tesla immediately quit. Instead of bringing a brilliant colleague into the fold and capitalizing on his creativity, Edison turned Tesla into a lifelong rival.

Once Tesla convinced Pittsburgh industrialist George Westinghouse to fund his research, it was war—AC versus DC. Edison launched a propaganda campaign to position AC technology as too dangerous to deploy. To drive his point home, he staged public electrocutions of dogs, horses, and even an elephant. The capper was the use of the world's first electric chair to execute a murderer, a technique that became known as "Westinghousing."

Bidding against Edison's company, the Westinghouse Corporation won the contract to illuminate the world's first electrified World's Fair, the Columbian Exposition in Chicago. Another huge win followed—the Tesla-designed AC hydroelectric power plant at Niagara Falls, used to power the entire city of Buffalo, New York. Ultimately, Edison only managed to delay the inevitable. As evidenced by your dusty CD collection, no amount of spin can protect a technology from obsolescence.

Had Edison not alienated Tesla, the two might have perfected the AC generator together and had a long, fruitful collaboration. But Edison let his emotions and his ego get in the way of his judgment, and the smear campaign he orchestrated became an unfortunate part of his legacy. This is a mistake that never seems to go out of style. In recent years, Boeing, Facebook, and Sanofi all took billion-dollar hits because they refused to admit they were wrong. This may feel good in the moment but it's neither noble nor strategic.

LIKABILITY

Albert Einstein's equation $E = mc^2$ challenged Newtonian physics and the concept of "ether," the undetectable mysterious matter that filled space, according to scientific theory at the dawn of the twentieth century. Scientists had come up with the concept of ether to explain questions around the nature of electricity, the movement of light, and even the concept of nothingness. As it turned out, however, ether was undetectable because it didn't exist! As radical as Einstein's theory was, it did not take long for his peers to come around. The press picked up on $E = mc^2$, and soon everyday people everywhere were reading about it in the newspaper.

How did Einstein get people to buy into his radical theory so quickly? Why is $E = mc^2$ the one mathematical formula most people know? Sure, Einstein was a genius and his math checked out, but what won him so many fans was his likability. Einstein was a great storyteller. His genius is in math and physics, but it is his ability to turn his work into a story that made him an icon. He built his personal brand by reducing complex concepts to their simple essence, as he himself said in his famous quote,

"If you can't explain it to a six-year-old, you don't understand it yourself."

There's no duplicating Einstein's personal charm—that unruly mop of hair, thick accent, bushy mustache, and blunt wit—but like Einstein, you can tap into your own storytelling ability to boost your likability with the person you are trying to convince.

Come Up with a Good Guy and a Bad Guy

The best stories have a hero and a villain. The bad guy doesn't have to be human—you can position a concept, problem, or pain point as the enemy. Setting up a shared problem as the villain on which to build your argument is a storytelling technique that can be very effective in business.

Know the Value of Validation—Agree Before You Disagree

The further apart you and the person you are trying to convince are in your opinions, the more important it is to demonstrate respect. Agree before you disagree. Use phrases like, "I get why you think that." "I understand how you reached that conclusion." "That idea makes a lot of sense." Saying that you understand someone's thought process does not necessarily mean you agree with their conclusions. You are simply validating their thinking, something people don't want to be questioned. Find little things to agree about when the other person is making their point. This helps soften them up enough to listen to what you have to say.

Don't Be the Smartest Person in the Room—Even If You Are

Make people feel good about themselves. There's a wrong way and a right way to be right. The wrong way could sabotage your pitch. The right way gets things done. Acknowledge that you appreciate the other person's knowledge and know-how. Find a way to weave some of their thinking and research into your pitch to demonstrate how their existing knowledge fits in with your new idea.

Understand That Not Everyone Is Going to Like You

Regardless of what your mom might think, you are always going to rub some people the wrong way. Even the most popular stars have their detractors. If you are not getting simpatico vibes from the person you are trying to convince, focus on your story. Just because they wouldn't invite you over for dinner doesn't mean you can't interest them in what you have to say.

REPEATABILITY

In popular music, it's called "the hook." In classical music, it's a theme or a leitmotif. We refer to a catchy tune as an earworm and complain when a song is "stuck in our heads."

Repeatability is what makes music memorable.

The principle of repeatability is an essential part of communication and convincing. From "Build That Wall" to "Build Back Better," we can all think of political catchphrases that have taken off and become popular tropes. Disciplined political operatives use these phrases over and over to drum them into people's brains, and political parties try to get all their members on board with the same wording. Before you know it, political junkies on Twitter are parroting those very same catchphrases.

Before you go in and pitch your idea, ask for a raise, or start a negotiation, think about the two or three most important points you want to make. Can you sum them up in a quick, memorable way? The wording doesn't have to be exact—you're not writing a slogan—but see if you can sneak in the argument more than once. Say you're asking for that raise, and you helped close a deal that won the company a fat new account. That's a great support point for your ask and one you need to include as part of your top-line pitch. Maybe you can reinforce it by bringing up something that happened during the negotiation or mentioning the great restaurant your team ate at to celebrate the win. That is more subtle than literally repeating that you had a big role in closing the deal, but when you walk out the door, that support point will stick with your boss.

We know our ideas can't be music to everyone's ears, and our convincing strategy is bound to strike the occasional dissonant note. When that happens, it's tempting to just focus on the positive and move on. Instead, see if you can pinpoint what aspect of your convincing strategy turned people off, so you don't make the same mistake twice.

KEY TAKEAWAYS

- Focus on delivering the right message, at the right time. That means factoring in the four essential elements of effective convincing: timing, believability, likability, and repeatability.
- The further apart you and the person you're trying to convince are in your opinions, the more important it is to demonstrate respect. Agree before you disagree. Use phrases like, "I get why you think that." Saying that you understand someone's thought process does not necessarily mean you agree with their conclusions. You are simply validating their thinking, something people don't want to be questioned.

PART THREE

APPLYING CONVINCING TECHNIQUES TO YOUR WORLD

CHAPTER 17

CONVINCING SITUATIONS IN BUSINESS

Congratulations! You now have a fully stocked arsenal of convincing skills to draw from. You are no longer falling into the trap of feeling the other person is unmovable. You don't rely on techniques that work only some of the time. Rather, you now know exactly how to adapt your approach to fit the person you are trying to convince.

Forensic Listening has become your go-to guide for getting to someone's Unstated Narrative quickly and effectively. Instead of just asking questions, you use high-level predictive statements to get others to reveal more about themselves willingly. You can immediately sort others into two convincing camps, fact-based or emotional, and adapt your style to their thought process.

You study a person's Pattern of Life (POL), body positioning, and Signature Personality Consistencies and Inconsistencies with the keen sense of an FBI special agent. When you start convincing others, you never lead with your strongest point. Instead, you move them along the Convincing Continuum and leave them with a cliffhanger to ponder as they move closer to being persuaded.

You now have everything you need to not just succeed, but also to strive for ever higher levels of success. As your convincing confidence builds, your ability to read people and situations at a glance will open a world of possibilities. People will seek you out for deals, leadership positions, and coveted board seats. You will confidently go after that promotion, job, or client that you previously thought was beyond your reach. You'll be invited to exclusive parties, events, speaking gigs, and other networking opportunities with top people in your field. You will be handpicked for plum projects and exciting client assignments. Moreover, your advice will be so coveted, you'll be pulled into the conversations at the highest levels. The skills you've acquired will enable you to dominate all challenging business situations.

Based on what you learned, we've developed a list of situations you may find yourself in. See what convincing tools we recommend to ensure a good outcome.

SITUATION 1: EVALUATING YOUR NEW TEAM AFTER GETTING PROMOTED

Thanks to your hard work, not to mention your superb convincing capabilities, you have earned a big promotion. Now you need to evaluate your new team so you know what they are capable of and how to best utilize their respective skills. If you're observant, you may pick up some clues regarding team dynamics, rivalries, trustworthiness, and more.

Convincing Tools to Use in Situation 1

Start by having a departmental meeting with everyone in your team in the room. You won't be able to do too much Forensic Note-Taking, since the purpose of the meeting is ostensibly for you to introduce yourself. Tell your direct reports a bit about you. Of course, you don't need to go into great detail—they have likely googled you by now—but maybe a bit about your last couple of positions, hobbies, family, and so on. You want them to see you as a well-rounded person who doesn't just live to work. If your predecessor moved on or retired and was beloved by the team, celebrate their achievements. (If your predecessor was let go for valid reasons, you may want to skip that part!) When you do this, you demonstrate confidence in your own leadership abilities.

After the initial intros (don't forget to go around the room so everyone knows they matter), flip the script! Ask the team to come back to you with written suggestions for improving the department. Do they have a passion project? Do they see missed opportunities? What do they think your departmental priorities should be? Not only will this exercise help you learn a lot about your department and new colleagues, but it will also generate goodwill by positioning you as a good listener who values everyone's opinion.

After the meeting, quickly write down your observations. Who talked the most? Who never opened their mouth? Who's sharing knowing glances? Who does the team seem to look up to and like? Who made the most practical sense? Who had creative ideas? Who seems to have a good institutional memory?

Anything you noticed could be helpful. Then wait for everyone's suggestions to come in, and you're sure to learn even more about your new team.

SITUATION 2: REPLACING A MICROMANAGER

You are an incoming new department head introducing yourself to your team. Your predecessor, Mark, was a martinet and a micromanager and your new staff is traumatized.

Convincing Tools to Use in Situation 2

Micromanagement usually is caused by the leader's doubt in their own ability and insecurity. When people are micromanaged, they live in fear of being wrong or corrected. That's why you must create an environment where people know their ideas will be supported and it's OK to fail from time to time. You want to show them you understand their mindset and, more specifically, their fears. You will want to prepare five to seven messages to move the traumatized team down the Convincing Continuum. Your statements and messaging must be about understanding and affirming the here and now and painting a bright picture of the future. As a leader, you are all about taking them to the next level.

Messages to Move the Team Forward

Message 1. "We can all agree that we need a better approach to managing the team so everyone feels more supported."

Message 2. "You are all professionals and being micromanaged is stifling and time-consuming."

Message 3. "While Mark's intentions were good, his style might not be right for everyone."

Message 4. "Let's work on ways I can support each of you individually to get the best results."

Give Them a Convincing Cliffhanger

Message 5. For example, you might say, "Based on industry research, self-motivated management is most effective. Please look at this *Harvard Business Review* article on the topic. I'd like to meet with each of you and discuss your suggestions to create a work environment where we can all thrive."

As a result of this strategic tactic, your team will feel seen and heard, and challenged to come up with solutions that will work for them. This process will convince the team you are a leader who will support and respect them.

You will use Targeted Validation and draw attention to areas that need improvement, clarify your expectations, and alleviate your team's fear of retribution. Being public and open regarding behaviors you like will be pivotal to moving people out of a fear-based culture. Use situational awareness to identify who the group has been looking to as their de facto leader, and strive to gain the support of that person as you engage your new team. That person could be a resource of institutional knowledge and a powerful ally for you.

SITUATION 3: GETTING SOMEONE TO COMPLETE A TASK

In this interaction, you are asking someone over whom you have no real managerial authority to complete a task critical to your success. Although you've interacted with them several times in the past, you still have difficulty knowing whether they will comply with your request.

Convincing Tools to Use in Situation 3

Consider what you want the other person to think, feel, and do.

- **Think.** You want this coworker to *think* that the project and its completion will help them. Be sure to point out how working with you will lead to their success, not yours.
- **Feel.** Working on this project, this person will *feel* positive about your work together and continue to work hard throughout the project, because you will purposefully praise their contribution in public or over a group email when the project is getting off the ground.
- **Do.** As a result of their renewed focus on completing the task based on how it could benefit them, they will be more motivated to *do* the project and comply with your request.

Make a business case with an outcome that benefits them. Think about interactions you've had with them that provided insight into what's important to them. If they are a fact-based thinker, use industry benchmarking reports, statistics, and data to illustrate how collaborating with you could benefit them and their career. If they are more emotional, appeal to their ambition by positioning the project as an opportunity and assure them that you will tout their contribution directly to your mutual supervisor.

SITUATION 4: SETTING A SALES TARGET

You are the supervisor, and you need your employees to adopt a new sales target. You know there is some resistance from your team regarding how you should go about achieving this goal. Due to unforeseen circumstances, the last sales target was not met, and you believe people's confidence in your leadership is waning.

Convincing Tools to Use in Situation 4

Any project that requires group buy-in requires increased effort on everyone's part. Meeting one-on-one with each member of the team and taking Forensic Notes will give you an advantage. As you ask questions about why they didn't hit their numbers and what can be done to achieve better results, you will be listening for way more than the content of their answers. You will be gauging their emotional state and paying attention to repeated themes and word choice, body positioning, and voice, pitch, tone, and cadence.

Listen for what they do not mention. This can be especially telling if there is one obvious point that never surfaces in any of the talks, such as their perception, however incorrect, that you may not be up to the challenges of your job. Sometimes you can determine the most important issue by looking at what they are vague about or what seems to make them uncomfortable. That's when you want to ask targeted follow-up questions. The answers you need likely reside in the areas they are reluctant to flesh out.

Next, meet with the team as a whole. This can be a standing meeting. Here is where you will practice the syncing method. First apologize to the group. Using the language uncovered in your interviews, give it back to them, and tell them you're sorry about missing the last quarter's goal. Apologizing, even when it is not your fault, creates a positive dopamine hit in the brain of the person you are apologizing to. Next, you will outline the actual steps, daily, weekly, and monthly it will take to reach the sales goal. Be sure to praise certain members of the group for their successes to date. Let the group know that this standing meeting will happen each morning for 10 minutes. The meeting will consist of:

1. Yesterday's progress
2. What is needed today
3. If possible, a success story about what someone in the group did to further the progress toward the goal

Business development executive Jamie Ninneman of SAP says that in his experience, some folks in corporate America treat information like a currency. For those types of people, Ninneman recommends surrounding the person you want to convince with other team members who are also validating your ideas and suggestions. By using Targeted Validation and Concert Convincing methods—you are effectively "surrounding them" with your ideas and they are more likely to adopt your idea, suggestion, or project.

Following this recipe will sync the brains of each team member and prep them for a successful workday.

SITUATION 5: ATTRACTING PEOPLE TO A VOLUNTARY PROFESSIONAL DEVELOPMENT CLASS

You are asking 25 colleagues to participate in a voluntary professional development opportunity. Your bosses will judge your ability to lead based on how many people participate. How do you come across to your coworkers on this type of email?

Convincing Tools to Use in Situation 5

Leverage the Majority Illusion by asking a handful of your team members to act as "idea brokers" before sharing the request with the entire team. Make the favor of backing your idea so easy they can't help but support you. Suggest that you will write their email to the group for them, backing up your professional development recommendation.

Remember to only ask people you know well, trust, and respect, because you should be ready to return the favor. To take it a step further, suggest specific ways you can reciprocate.

SITUATION 6: MEETING A NEW BOSS

There's a new sheriff in town—your boss has been replaced. You are going in for an introductory one-on-one.

Convincing Tools to Use in Situation 6

Identifying the new boss's Unstated Narrative will be crucial. Understanding what they value will give you a glimpse into what they really want to achieve and what is important to them. When you can identify that, you can help them achieve their goal and demonstrate that you understand them and are on their side. As a current employee, you can be a good source of institutional knowledge. Share your ideas on how to make the department more efficient, grow certain accounts, pick up some new business, and so on. Do not start dissing any of your colleagues. You don't want to be seen as a gossip or a backstabber. Don't bug the boss unless you have something significant to say—you don't want to be one of those sycophants who pops in to the new boss's office five times a day. Any secure, intelligent manager will see right through that.

To impress the boss, you can come up with an industry trend you see coming around the corner using the Back to the Future Framework. Use credible support data to lay out what you saw in the past and what is happening now, and outline what you think will happen in the future. You can discuss this prediction with them and position yourself as a forward-thinker.

SITUATION 7: INAPPROPRIATE JOB INTERVIEW QUESTIONS

You are at a job interview and the interviewer is asking probing, inappropriate questions about your current company. You want the job, but you don't want to reveal anything you shouldn't.

Convincing Tools to Use in Situation 7

Hostage negotiators are constantly evaluating the words and lines of discussion being chosen by the hostage taker or person in crisis. Certain words and topics may clue a negotiator in to the true motivations or real fears and desires not fully expressed by the hostage taker. Chip might have wanted to get a hostage taker to expand upon some words. For example, he might have asked, "You said you want a plane. Where are you planning on going?"

Conversely, any topic that will not ultimately serve as a peaceful resolution of the person in crisis is an area to avoid or reframe. For example, during one negotiation, the suspect was agitated and kept asking for drugs. To redirect him, Chip acknowledged the request. "OK, you mention wanting this certain drug several times. I know it must be frustrating not getting it. Can you tell me what it is like for you when you take this drug?" This response shows empathy by acknowledging their desire for this drug. At the same time, Chip was moving the suspect off the demand and changing the topic without being overt about it.

Similarly, let's say your job interviewer has drifted from the topic that you want them to pursue and is now going down a line of questions seeking intel on your current place of work. Not only are you dealing with the stress of a job interview, but now you must figure out why this is happening and how can you redirect this line of questions to your advantage.

Maybe he wants to know if you would disrespect an employer by airing dirty laundry. Perhaps he's testing you to see how you handle an uncomfortable situation. It's even possible the company has no intention of hiring you and has only brought you in to pump you for information. You finally conclude nothing good will come from answering these questions. Now you are going to dial into this interviewer and use Reverse the Focus and add in tension, a Forer statement, and confidence.

"These questions make me feel like you are asking me to provide some internal information about my current employer. I want to make sure I'm not giving out information I shouldn't." All of this was a tension add.

Next you are going to reverse the focus. "Maybe there is something else I can answer that might help your evaluation of me without giving away too much?" Wait for an answer here.

Then follow with a Forer statement like, "You know in the short time we have talked, I get the impression you are the one they call on to get results. Am I right?"

Now you will do well to add in some confidence using virtue signaling here. Clearly, anyone who would bad-mouth a current employer would also do the same to the next employer. Confidently state, "I am sure you understand my personal code of integrity does not allow me to reveal anything improper about my employer."

SITUATION 8: DEALING WITH A JADED CUSTOMER SERVICE AGENT

Your flight's been cancelled and you're on terminal hold, waiting to rebook and listening to the worst music on loop. Finally, the phone rings and the customer service agent picks up. You're already doing a slow boil, and you sense an attitude coming from the very person that's supposed to help you book a new flight. Now you have a few options:

- Match their attitude
- Escalate the situation
- Display empathy for your future self

Convincing Tools to Use in Situation 8

In this example, empathy for your future self isn't about whining "poor me." It's about understanding who holds the power right now (*hint:* it isn't you). If the service agent senses anger in your voice, they could "accidentally" cut you off so you have to wait another 30 minutes, or book you for tomorrow so you have to check in to a hotel for the night. Focus on the pitch, tone, and cadence of your voice to convey empathy for the customer service agent who rarely gets any from irate customers. Additionally, find something you can validate about the customer service person's experience, like: "I am sorry (pause, pause, pause). I know you must get so many of these calls and you are just trying to help."

If you weren't angry and frustrated, you might feel empathy for that beleaguered service agent. The cancellation and 30 minutes of holding are not their fault. Chances are they've been dealing with irate customers for hours. Then again, that's their job, and besides, empathy is a tall order when your amygdala has been hijacked and you're using your primitive brain. Faking empathy won't get you very far. That agent doesn't owe you anything. You are as anonymous to them as the last person they rebooked, no matter how hard you try to pretend that you feel bad about their stressful day. Chances are, you won't sound authentic.

Focusing on your frustration and inconvenience won't help you get your flight rebooked. You don't want to have sat through 30 minutes of hold music in vain.

SITUATION 9: GETTING A BIGGER BITE OF THE BUDGET FOR YOUR PROJECTS

You're one of 12 department heads all reporting to the same senior vice president and all vying for a bigger piece of the budget to fund their teams' projects. How do you get your department a bigger piece of the pie?

Convincing Tools to Use in Situation 9

Present your business case using the Convincing Continuum. Rather than walk in, hat in hand, and ask for more money, start in the latitude of agreement. Make a point you and the boss can both agree upon, such as the positive contributions your department has made to the company's reputation, bottom line, or internal organization. Perhaps you can use the Reach-Back technique and bolster your case by using something your boss has said or is known to believe. Don't make this about your personal success, but about your department as a whole—you're asking for money for your department, not a raise. Do a little future-casting and paint a picture of what a bigger budget could allow you to achieve. Your boss will likely agree to think about your request and get back to you—leave them with a convincing cliffhanger to ponder overnight. Plant a touch of fear, uncertainty, and doubt. What are the potential consequences of your department being underfunded? Share something about your department that helps support your request and is likely new information for your boss.

SITUATION 10: GETTING YOUR BOSS TO ACT IN A CRISIS SITUATION

One of your team members is being sexually harassed by a senior manager. HR has spoken to the senior manager about the situation, and the manager has toned it down, only to pick a new target. The first victim has quit, and you've heard rumblings about a possible lawsuit. You think this has the makings of a serious PR crisis, but your CEO is hesitant to call in a crisis communications expert. How do you convince him?

Convincing Tools to Use in Situation 10

How does fear affect your CEO's decision-making? In this case, it appears that he is turtling, withdrawing rather than making a critical decision. Nudging him out of denial will require tact on your part, especially if there are more people in the room than just the two of you. His emotional driver appears to be a desire for security. He is likely not entirely sure of himself and needs to feel respected by the team, so this is no time to get caught up in "the saga of your righteousness" and possibly embarrass him. Instead, try a little future-casting. He is already nervous about the situation and afraid to make a decision. Your task is to make him realize that the potential consequences of doing nothing are actually scarier than hiring outside help. Label his emotions and use the trust narrative to make him realize you understand and are on his side. Say things like, "I know you're not too pleased with this situation," or "Of course this is a tough decision, and it has to be hard for you." Use the Dial-in Method to emphasize that you are listening and the Reach-Back technique to make him feel good about himself and his past decisions.

SITUATION 11: INTERVIEWING A POTENTIAL HIRE

You urgently need to fill a position in your department. You're understaffed and your team is overworked. After weeks of unimpressive candidates, you're down to two finalists. How do you make the right choice?

Convincing Tools to Use in Situation 11

If the candidates had to go through several interviews to get to you, and this is your first encounter, use the 22-Second Reading to get a quick feel for them. Ask yourself the critical question:

Is the candidate trying to impress me or make a connection? Most interviewees will try to impress you, but the one who is working to connect and find common ground is revealing superior communication skills. If they proactively ask *you* questions before you ask if they have any, it shows that they are curious and engaged. The questions they ask could reveal a lot about their emotional drivers. Do they seem motivated by security, or are they more interested in professional growth? Calibrate their confidence—remember, the magic number is 4 out of 5. An overconfident person could be compensating for being underqualified, or they might come off as cocky and not fit in with the rest of the team. A person who seems a little hesitant or understated may not be assertive enough to succeed in certain jobs unless it's a position where quiet competence will do just fine. If you find yourself feeling particularly enthusiastic about a candidate and you believe they have other options, try using the Frank technique: Tell them a story about a big win, new product, or company event and bring them into the story, saying things like, "Wait 'til you see for yourself!" or "You'll love him, he's a legend around here."

SITUATION 12: YOU'RE A NEW ENTREPRENEUR WALKING THE CONVENTION FLOOR

Going up and down the aisles handing out business cards may help you get your steps in, but it's not the most effective way to drum up new business. So what do you do?

Convincing Tools to Use in Situation 12

First of all, understand that while you may make some great contacts, trade shows are sales events, not networking sessions.

You are not there to make friends. Everyone there, including you, is there to sell something, whether it's a product, a service, or their particular skill set. You will be doing the 22-Second Reading a lot, after which you will likely quickly move on to the next person. On the other hand, if a conversation continues for a few minutes, you have an opportunity to make a connection. Use the Dial-in Method, subtly of course, to signal that you are listening. If you're a good storyteller, make like Frank and bring the listener into your story but keep it about business, your career, or your industry. If you are working the show with a partner, so much the better. You can tout each other's accomplishments, which is less awkward than selling yourself. Adele did this quite successfully after launching her PR firm. She met a marketing person on the convention floor who had also just started her own business. The two women hit it off and decided to walk the show together. They even wrote each other's talking points so they could sell each other more effectively! Both came away with some new clients and a couple of shared ones!

PRACTICE NEW CONVINCING SKILLS

The preceding examples demonstrate how you can use your new convincing skills in real-life situations. However, it will take a little time for this to become second nature. Every time you apply what you have learned to a new situation, you will get a little better at convincing.

Practice doesn't make perfect—it makes perfect connections in your brain. When someone learns a new skill, they lay down a "neural framework" to be able to improve on certain tasks in the future. That framework is transmitted over what neuroscientists call "action potentials" from one neuron to another. Think of how you learned to ride a bicycle as a kid. You may have fallen over and skinned a knee a few times, but eventually that perfect balance became instinctive until you felt almost one with your bike. As you do tasks over and over again, you start to improvise and build on your skills, adding your own approach and style as your brain forms new pathways.

When you become more convincing, you are helping move the world forward and create the future. All the most world-changing ideas began with somebody convincing others to do great things. We hope you use the tools in this book to change your life, personally and professionally. And we are convinced you will.

NOTES

Introduction

1. Margaret Echelbarger, Kayla Good, and Alex Shaw. *Judgment and Decision Making*, vol. 15, no. 6, November 2020, pp. 959–971.

Chapter 2

1. Scott Magids, Alan Zorfas, and Daniel Leemon. "The New Science of Customer Emotions," *Harvard Business Review*, November 2015.
2. Sigal Barsade and Olivia A. O'Neil. "Manage Your Emotional Culture," *Harvard Business Review*, February 2016.

Chapter 3

1. Personal interview.
2. Brian Luntz. "Scientist Program Mice to Be Friends Using Neuron Stimulating Brain Implants," IFLScience, May 11, 2021.
3. Simon Sinek, David Mead, and Peter Docker. *Find Your Why: A Practical Guide for Discovering Purpose for You and Your Team*. Portfolio. 2017.

Chapter 4

1. https://www8.gsb.columbia.edu/video/videos/how-influence-people-negotiation-vs-persuasion-skills.

2. https://smartypantsmagazineforkids.com/2022/09/28/andrew-carnegie-and-the-elephant-who-crossed-the-bridge/.

Chapter 5

1. Matthew Hutson. *Scientific American*, April 4, 2017. https://www.scientificamerican.com/author/matthew-hutson/.
2. Personal interview.
3. https://www.pnas.org/doi/10.1073/pnas.2118548119.

Chapter 6

1. https://doi.org/10.2201/nonlin.003.01.001.
2. David Burkus. *Under New Management: How Leading Organizations Are Upending Business as Usual*. Harper Business. June 2017.
3. https://www.jstor.org/stable/10.1086/421787.
4. Zig Ziglar. *See You at the Top: 25th Anniversary Edition*. June 2000.
5. https://onlinelibrary.wiley.com/doi/full/10.1111/ecin.12882.
6. https://www.youtube.com/watch?v=P8Pu9j5oo6k.
7. https://www.eofire.com/podcast/.

Chapter 7

1. https://www.theatlantic.com/health/archive/2015/02/this-is-your-brain-on-magic/385468/.
2. https://parade.com/50115/parade/interview-with-criss-angel/.
3. https://psychologyconcepts.com/barnum-effect-or-forer-effect/.
4. https://www.forbes.com/sites/giovannirodriguez/2017/07/21/this-is-your-brain-on-storytelling-the-chemistry-of-modern-communication/?sh=676ae19ac865.
5. https://www.researchgate.net/publication/232543099_Everyday_mind_reading_Understanding_what_other_people_think_and_feel.

Chapter 8

1. https://www.pnas.org/content/107/32/14425.
2. https://www.cell.com/current-biology/home.

Chapter 9

1. https://www.cbinsights.com/research/what-is-psychographics/.

Chapter 10

1. Personal interview.
2. https://nypost.com/2018/12/14/this-is-exactly-how-long-you-have-to-make-a-good-first-impression/.
3. https://www.drjudyho.com/stop-self-sabotage.

4. https://www.pnas.org/doi/10.1073/pnas.1920484117.

Chapter 11

1. Personal interview.
2. Personal interview.
3. https://workforceinstitute.org/.
4. https://www.bls.gov/opub/ted/2021/quits-rate-of-2-9-percent-in-august-2021-an-all-time-high.htm.

Chapter 12

1. https://www.azquotes.com/quote/552174.
2. https://brainworldmagazine.com/the-myth-of-multitasking/.
3. https://doi.org/10.1016/j.neuron.2006.11.009.
4. Gary Noesner. *Stalling for Time*. Random House. 2010.

Chapter 13

1. https://www.quotes.net/quote/51459.
2. https://img.en25.com/Web/CPP/Conflict_report.pdf.
3. https://procurementtactics.com/negotiation-quotes/.
4. https://www.ted.com/talks/mihaly_csikszentmihalyi_flow_the_secret_to_happiness?language=en.
5. https://hbr.org/2008/09/how-pixar-fosters-collective-creativity.
6. https://hbr.org/2021/08/why-are-we-so-emotional-about-money.
7. https://www.pbs.org/newshour/economy/making-sense/money-habits-are-set-by-age-7-teach-your-kids-the-value-of-a-dollar-now.

Chapter 14

1. https://www.wired.com/2007/03/security-matters0322/.
2. https://www.npr.org/2010/12/06/131734718/just-breathe-body-has-a-built-in-stress-reliever.

Chapter 15

1. https://www.cnn.com/videos/us/2018/02/19/1995-john-f-kennedy-jr-remembering-jfk-larry-king-sot.cnn.
2. https://www.fastcompany.com/90733407/the-dos-and-donts-of-creating-your-company-vision.

Chapter 16

1. https://www.psychologytoday.com/us/blog/the-social-thinker/201401/why-new-year-day-s-is-the-worst-day-start-your-resolution.

INDEX

ABOUT THE AUTHORS

Adele Gambardella-Cehrs is the cofounder of the Convincing Company. Honored as a "Woman Who Means Business" by the *Washington Business Journal*, she has served as PR strategist, corporate counsel, and crisis management consultant for such clients as Facebook, Johnson & Johnson, Samsung, Lockheed Martin, SAP, and President Joe Biden.

Prior to cofounding Convincing Company, Adele owned a Top 20 PR firm in Washington, DC. She has acted as a spokesperson for a variety of Fortune 100 companies, ranging from DuPont to Lockheed Martin to Verizon. As a publicist, she landed interviews for her clients on *Good Morning America*, the *Today Show*, and the *New York Times*. Adele started her career as a journalist for *George* magazine and the *Asbury Park Press*. She maintains her writing chops as a contributor to the *Wall Street Journal* and *Entrepreneur* magazine.

Adele has addressed a broad range of companies and associations as a professional speaker. Her presentations to the United Nations have been broadcast worldwide. She has taught crisis communications and business at Princeton, Cornell, George Mason, and Georgetown universities.

Adele has helped hundreds of business owners make their mark as thought leaders in their respective industries. As a corporate fixer, she works with C-suite executives in Fortune 500 companies to break through the clutter and build or repair their brands.

Chip Massey, a former FBI hostage negotiator and special agent, puts the high-stakes negotiation skills he refined during his 20-plus years in law enforcement to work for today's business leaders. As a consultant and cofounder of the Convincing Company, Chip teaches his clients to apply the bureau's sophisticated negotiation techniques to any business situation. He has worked with entities ranging from technology startups to C-suite executives at Fortune 500 companies like Facebook, Samsung, and Goldman Sachs.

Over the course of his career, Chip has helped the CIA track down spies, lead high-profile criminal cases, and investigate the September 11th terrorist attack. In the New York field office, he led the crisis negotiations teams in all five boroughs. In addition to the techniques he learned at Quantico, Chip taps into the interpersonal skills he perfected during his prior career as a pastor. He was often the first person parishioners consulted in challenging, high-stress situations. When Rev. Massey became Agent Massey, the empathy and understanding he developed as a man of the cloth were an invaluable addition to his FBI toolkit.

Chip is a natural communicator and teacher who has instructed FBI agents, police officers, and other federal officials on hostage negotiation techniques, de-escalation, and other law enforcement issues. Additionally, he has taught thousands of students at West Point, Princeton, Cornell, Columbia, and other high-profile colleges.